THE 7 PREP STEPS

Seven Essential Steps to *REAL* Emergency Preparedness

by

Marcello Surjopolos

Preparedness Expert & Trainer

www.7PrepSteps.com

ISBN 979-8636022626

Printed in the United States of America

TABLE OF CONTENTS

WELCOME!!
(AND Congratulations!)

You're about to learn the 7 steps to *REAL* Emergency Preparedness. By taking the time to prepare yourself and your loved ones for crisis the right way, you're doing what less than 1% of the population will EVER do. The peace of mind you'll get will be priceless!

As I began this 7PrepSteps workbook, I faced a large challenge: how to create a preparedness workbook that's complete and comprehensive enough to fit most every crisis, and yet, at the same time, not get so extreme in ideas and action items that a person, family, or group could never achieve all of them in one lifetime.

I believe I did it! - something simple to follow and implement but complete enough that even people well-versed in preparedness will find inside little nuggets of golden wisdom they never fully considered. (For even deeper concepts, visit the www.7PrepSteps.com video course.)

The *7 Prep Steps* will save you months, if not years, of research time, and THOUSANDS of dollars in costly mistakes I had to make to know what I know today. You get to stand on my shoulders and see so much further than you could without this course.

The 7 Prep Steps is organized, <u>in order of priority</u>, into 7 sections (see below). You'll begin with the first, then progress to the next and the next, until you've completed this workbook.

1. **Risk Assessment** (understanding and preparing for your top risks)
2. **72-Hour Emergency Preparedness** (survival for the first 3 days)
3. **Water Preparedness** (emergency water survival over time)
4. **Food Preparedness** (your short and long-term food needs)
5. **Meet Your Other Needs** (e.g., heat, shelter, electricity, sanitation, tools, etc.)
6. **Maintain Your Standard of Living** (financial reserves and extra supplies)
7. **Help Others Prepare** (keeping your supplies secure and taking care of loved ones)

Each section is a mixture of concepts, ideas, and checklists that allow you to skip around or combine teachings to fit your individual goals and needs.

Whether you're preparing for tough economic times, a job loss, a pandemic, natural or man-made disasters, or any other crisis situation, I challenge you to do something today!

> I CHALLENGE you to do something today!

Get started, either alone or in a family or group, mark up this workbook, circle sections that speak to you, take notes, and then apply what you learn. Finish the course! You'll be glad you did!! And, remember...

IT'S BETTER TO BE PREPARED A YEAR EARLY, THAN EVEN ONE DAY TOO LATE.

So, let's get started!

Lessons From Hurricane Sandy

OVERCOMING THE NORMALCY BIAS

The Normalcy (or Normality) Bias

def: An idealization that because something hasn't happened in the past, the chance of it happening in the future is *unrealistic* or *unimaginable*. It's a sense of denial that leads people to *underestimate* or *minimalize* both the possibilities of a catastrophe happening and the danger posed to their health, safety, and security (or that of their loved ones).

The Normalcy Bias is probably the BIGGEST reason people don't prepare for emergencies and the cause of more fatalities in crises than any other reason.

In October of 2012, "Super" Hurricane Sandy, known as the largest Atlantic hurricane on record at that time, swept across the eastern United States and parts of the Caribbean taking the lives of over 230 people and leaving nearly 75 billion dollars in damage. In the United States alone, the most severe destruction was caused in New York and New Jersey.

Experience is the best teacher, *but it doesn't always have to be our own experiences* that teach us. So, to begin this workbook, let's take time to understand the unique experience and the insight of someone who lived through such a catastrophe.

A few weeks after Hurricane Sandy hit, one of the survivors (attributed to Frank Ostmann) wrote an email that quickly circulated around the globe. His viewpoints are priceless...

Things I learned From Hurricane Sandy

1. The excitement and coolness wear off around day 3.

2. You are never really prepared to go weeks without power, heat, water, etc. Never!

3. Yes, it can happen to you.

4. Just because your generator runs like a top, does not mean it's producing electricity.

5. If you do not have water stored up, you are in trouble. (A couple of cases of bottled water is "NOT" water storage.)

6. You should have as much fuel as water (propane, gas, kerosene, firewood, fire starter, kindling, paper, etc.)

7. Even the smallest little thing that you get from the store should be stocked up (spark plug for the generator, BBQ lighter, etc.).

8. If you are not working, chances are nobody else is either.

9. I was surprised how quickly normal social behavior goes out the window. I am not talking about someone cutting in line at the grocery store. (3 people were killed at gas stations within 50 miles of my home; I did not say 3 fights broke out; 3 people were killed.)

10. Cash is king (all the money in your savings means nothing).

11. Stored water can taste nasty.

12. You eat a lot more food when you are cold.

13. You need more food than you think if your kids are out of school for 2 weeks.

14. Kids do not like washing their face in cold water.

15. Your 1972 Honda civic gets to the grocery store as well as your 2012 Escalade... but the Honda allows money left over for heat, food, water, a generator, firewood, a backup water pump, ... (you get the idea).

16. The electrical grid is way more fragile than I thought.

17. Think of the things that are your comfort, your escape, a cup of hot chocolate, a glass of milk and a Ding Dong before bed, etc. Stock up on those too. You will need that comfort after day 3.

18. You quickly become the guy in the neighborhood who knows how to wire a generator to the electrical panel, directly wire the furnace to a small generator, or get the well pump up and running on inverter power, or you are the guy whose Master's degree in Accounting suddenly means nothing. (Love you Steve!)

19. A woman who can cook a fine meal by candlelight over the BBQ or open fire is worth her weight in gold. And women, whose weight in gold would not add up to much, usually die off first. Sorry skinny women.

20. It takes a lot of firewood to keep a fire going all day and into the evening for heat.

21. All the food storage in the world means nothing if your kids won't eat it.

22. You might be prepared to take care of your children and their needs, but what about when the neighborhood children start to show up at your door?

23. Some people shut down in an emergency. There is nothing that you can do about that.

24. Your town, no matter how small, is entirely dependent on outside sources of everything (if supply trucks stop rolling in due to road damage, gas shortages, or anything else, you could be without for a long time).

25. In an emergency, men stock up on food, women stock up on toilet paper.

26. I was surprised how many things run on electricity!

27. You can never have enough matches.

28. Although neighbors can be a great resource, they can also be a huge drain on your emergency storage. You need to know how you are going to handle that. It is really easy to be Bob, the guy who shares on Day 3, not so easy on Day 11. This is just reality speaking.

29. Give a man a fish he eats for that day, teach a man to fish and he will never be hungry again. Now I get it.

30. All of the expensive clothes in the closet mean nothing if they don't keep you warm.

31. Same goes for shoes... Love you Honey!!!!

32. You cannot believe the utility companies. They are run by politicians!! Or so it seems.

33. Anything that you depend on someone else for is not available anymore.

34. Quote "A man with a chainsaw that knows how to use it, is a thing of beauty." lol

35. Most folks don't have any emergency storage. They run to Wal-Mart and get water and batteries and then fill their tubs with water. That is it. A lucky few will get a case of ramen and a box of pop tarts. That will be your neighbor's supply (especially if you live outside of Utah).

36. Fathers, all the money you have ever made means nothing if you can't keep your kids warm.

37. Mothers, everything you have ever done for your kids is forgotten if your kids are hungry.

38. You really do not want to be the "Unprepared Parents." The kids turn on you pretty quick.

39. Small solar charging gadgets will keep you in touch. Most work pretty well it seems.

40. Most things don't take much power to operate (computers, phones, radios, TV, lights).

41. Some things take a ton of power to operate (fridge, toaster, freezer, hot plate, microwave).

42. When it gets dark at 4:30 pm, the nights are really long without power.

43. Getting out of the house is very important, even if it is cold outside. Make your home the semi-warm place to come home to, and not the cold prison that you are stuck in.

44. Someone in your family must play or learn to play guitar.

45. Things that disappeared never to be seen again for a very long time: fuel of all kinds, matches, lighters of any kind, toilet paper, paper plates, plastic forks and knives, batteries (didn't really see a need for them...Flashlights??? I guess), milk, charcoal, spark plugs

(generators), 2-stroke motor oil (chainsaws), anything that could be used to wire a generator to the house, extension cords, medicines (Tylenol, Advil, cold medicine, etc.)
46. There was a strange peace to knowing all I had to do each day was keep my family safe, warm, and fed, but my peace was someone else's panic.

There were also many things that were not learned from hurricane Sandy, but reinforced. Those things were the importance of my family and their love and support, especially my lovely wife, that my Heavenly Father is really in charge, period, and finally that I am very thankful for the upbringing and experiences that have taught me and brought me to where I am... wherever that is...hahahaha.

As you read Frank's email above, hopefully you put yourself in his place to some degree. Maybe you even began considering how you can better prepare yourself for unexpected emergency situations that could happen to you and your family someday. If so, good!

As we proceed to PrepStep #1 (the Risk Assessment section), my goal is to help to start breaking down what's called the "Normalcy Bias" in you.

Simply because something bad hasn't happened to us in the past, we struggle to believe anything "that bad" will happen to us in the future. We remain indifferent to emergency preparedness (until the evening news scares us enough, that is), thanks to the Normalcy Bias.

This lack of preparedness is the biggest reason for injury and loss of life in any catastrophe.

In preparation for this book, I surveyed several random people to understand how they truly felt about the need for emergency preparedness. I found that most people weren't concerned, but those who had previously experienced some type of crisis, directly or indirectly, were.

For example, people who had lost their jobs, were more concerned about job security, and people affected by the stock market crash of 1929 or even 2008, tended to hoard more things, save more money, and have a greater desire to get out of debt.

On the flipside, people, even in the most emergency prone places in the United States, who hadn't yet experienced a large earthquake, flood, hurricane, tornado, sink hole, fire, drought, mudslide, or anything else common to their location, didn't seem to care much about emergency preparedness. They wouldn't even spend a mere $20 to put together a very simple emergency 72-hour grab-n-go kit for themselves or their family members.

In 2006, a *Time* magazine article explored reasons why people won't prepare for disasters. It cited that 91% of Americans live in places "at a moderate-to-high" risk of natural disaster, yet many of those who were polled explained that emergency preparation was not a priority since they believed they were *not* at risk. Reasons given for lack of preparation included "it won't happen to me" and "if it happens to me, it won't be that bad."... (*Time*, "Why We Don't Prepare for Disaster," Aug. 20, 2006). Don't be found victim to this type of thinking!

So, let's get started with breaking down *your own* Normalcy Bias. Continue on...

PrepStep #1
RISK ASSESSMENT

Be Prepared... the meaning of the motto is that a scout must prepare himself by previous thinking out and practicing how to act on any accident or emergency so that he is never taken by surprise.
- Robert Baden-Powell

TYPES OF
EMERGENCY SITUATIONS

There are only two types of emergencies: *natural* and *man-made*. Yet, of these two, come infinite combinations of disaster situations, from hurricanes, earthquakes, floods, pandemics, and wildfires, to civil unrest, economic downturns, terrorist attacks, and chemical spills.

Crisis situations also come in all shapes and sizes as well as in intensities and durations.

Some emergencies last only a few minutes and others, several years. Being "prepared" not only involves understanding the inherent dangers of each type of crisis, but also having the right skills, the right supplies, and enough of them to last the duration of the emergency.

The object of PrepStep#1 (the Risk Assessment section) is to help you better understand the emergency threats that pertain specifically to you and then lay the groundwork for the rest of the 7 Prep Steps, so by the end of this workbook, you are completely prepared, the right way.

You can't really prepare the right way, though, unless you *really* know what you're preparing for. This means you need to take your risk assessment seriously, take notes, and do the work.

There are several types of emergencies we'll cover in this section, but that doesn't mean you have to study all of them if you don't want to.

For example, if you don't live close to a large body of water and you don't really travel much, tsunamis probably aren't that important for you to prepare for, right? But, if you want to study more about tsunamis, go for it!

You can skip sections that don't matter to you, and study more in depth those that do. Read as much as you feel you should - the more you know, the better.

The 7PrepSteps is a course of action. Let's get onto your first exercise...

EXERCISE ONE

Review the most common Natural and Man-Made Disasters in PrepStep #1 and pick **at least 3** emergency situations that you think pertain to you. If you aren't sure if an emergency situation pertains to you, pick it just in case. You can rule it out later.

My recommendation is that everyone going through this course should at minimum include the "FIRES" section and the "MAN-MADE DISASTER" sections into your studies.

At the end of each disaster section there will be a worksheet. You can fill these out at any time to decide if a crisis situation is important enough for you to focus on it. Here's an example:

PREPARATION EXERCISE

After reading this section, what are some things you would like to do to better prepare yourself, your family, or your group for fire hazards? (write in the section below)

How probable is this crisis a threat to you?
(✔one): ☐0 ☐1 ☐2 ☐3 ☐4 ☐5 ☐6 ☐7 ☐8 ☐9 ☐10
How long might this crisis last for you?
(✔one): ☐3days ☐3wks ☐3mos ☐6mos ☐1yr ☐+yrs
Possible nearby threats that concern you:
_____

First of all, rate 0-10 (10 = Extremely Likely) how **probable** it is that that crisis might someday occur to you at home or in your travels. If the probability is a 7 or higher, then you should focus on that emergency situation as part of your risk assessment preparations.

You'll study each emergency situation you picked and really get a deep understanding of each one. You'll need to understand how you should prepare to survive for days, weeks, months, or even years, if needs be.

Most crisis situations fall into 4 categories:

>   **Short-Term Crisis** (Up to 3 days)
>   **Major Crisis** (Over 3 Days and Up to 3 Months)
>   **Long-Term Crisis** (Over 3 Months and Up to 1 Year)
>   **Lifestyle Change** (More than a Year)

For each crisis situation, decide how long you would like to be prepared for. This will help you in PrepSteps #2-6, so you know what supplies to store up and what skills you'll need to develop.

As part of each emergency section, list any additional threats near your home, school, or work that **concern** you (like potential landslides, wildfires, nuclear plants, chemical spills, flooding, gangs, rioting, etc.). You'll want to prepare for these as well.

As you study each crisis, create a **list of action items** you would like to do to better prepare yourself, your family, or your group for each different emergency situation.

NATURAL DISASTERS

Earthquakes

Earthquakes are more powerful than you think and can affect you even if you live far away from earthquakes zones. Take for example the 1964 Alaskan earthquake that shook most of mainland Alaska. Its 9.2 magnitude was the most powerful to ever hit U.S. soil.

For about 4 minutes, the ground rose up and down. Ports were ruptured, roads torn apart, transportation limited, towns wrecked, and thousands of aftershocks and hundreds of mudslides, sinkholes, and submarine slumps were found spread throughout.

Even for people that didn't live in Alaska, the earthquakes effects were felt thousands of miles away. Forty-seven of the fifty U.S. states registered the earthquake. Over 1,200 miles to the southeast, the world-famous Space Needle in Seattle, Washington, swayed back and forth. Tsunamis caused by the earthquake resulted in damage and deaths in Oregon and California. Water sloshed as far away as Texas and Louisiana. In the end, there were 129 deaths and $Billions in damage.

Just like most countries around the world, much of the United States currently lies within an earthquake territory to some degree. Take for example the list below. Here are the states that have experienced at least one 3+ magnitude earthquake in the last ±100 years:

Alabama (5.1)
Alaska (9.2)
Arizona (5.6)
Arkansas (4.7)
California (7.9)
Colorado (5.3)
Georgia (4.5)
Hawaii (7.9)
Idaho (6.9)
Illinois (5.4)
Indiana (4.6)
Kentucky (5.2)
Louisiana (4.2)
Maine (5.1)

Massachusetts Coast (3.6)
Michigan (4.6)
Minnesota (4.6)
Mississippi (4.6)
Montana (7.3)
Nebraska (5.1)
Nevada (7.2)
New Hampshire (5.5)
New Jersey (5.3)
New Mexico (5.1)
New York (5.8)
North Carolina (5.2)
North Dakota (5.5)
Ohio (5.4)

Oklahoma (5.6)
Oregon (6.8)
Pennsylvania (5.2)
Rhode Island (3.5)
South Carolina (4.4)
South Dakota (4.0)
Tennessee (4.5)
Texas (5.8)
Utah (6.6)
Vermont (4.2)
Virginia (5.8)
Washington (7.1)
West Virginia (4.5)
Wyoming (6.5)

Focusing on the United States alone, here are some of the most noted earthquake hot spots:

California – You can't live in the San Francisco, Los Angeles, Palm Springs, or most anywhere in California without feeling earthquakes to some degree on a regular basis. The San Andreas Fault extends 810 miles through California. Known as the "Big One," California is expecting around an 8-magnitude earthquake sometime in the near future.

Oregon and Washington – 50 miles off the coast of Oregon and Washington lies the Cascadia Subduction Zone that spans 680 miles and is capable of producing level 9 earthquakes that are 30 times more powerful than the San Andreas fault in California can produce. In fact, this earthquake threat is known as the "Really Big One."

Hawaii – Since 1868, there have been seven quakes of magnitude 6.2 or greater, like the 6.7 in 2006 that caused $250 million in damage.

Utah – Around every 300 years, Utah experiences a large earthquake (7.0+ magnitude), and it has been over 300 years since the last one. This would affect more than 1 million people living in what is called the Wasatch Front.

Idaho – Idaho is one of the most active states as far as the number of recorded earthquakes each year.

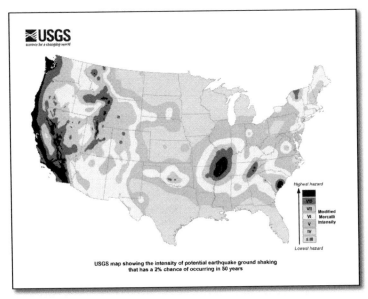

USGS map showing the intensity of potential earthquake ground shaking that has a 2% chance of occurring in 50 years

Wyoming – Mostly from faults and magma movement not visible on the surface, Wyoming is a "hotbed" for earthquake activity. There have been earthquakes in every county of the state over the last 120 years.

Missouri, Illinois, Kentucky, Tennessee, and Arkansas – In 1811-12, New Madrid, Missouri, experienced 3 large earthquakes (±8-magnitude each), which were felt over an area 2 million square miles wide. If similar earthquakes occurred today, there would be considerable damage in the surrounding large cities found within Missouri, Illinois, Kentucky, Tennessee, and Arkansas, that weren't there 200 years ago.

Earthquakes are quite prevalent and more widespread than we give them credit. No matter where you live, search the Internet or local records to understand how an earthquake may impact your city or state, even if it's in a neighboring state.

Large earthquakes are notorious for creating panic, food shortages, loss of electricity, communication, running water, natural gas, gasoline, or Internet for weeks, if not months. Banks may close, hospitals may be overloaded, and roads may be damaged, which could limit transportation and relief supplies.

So, what can you do to prepare?

BEFORE AN EARTHQUAKE

1. Have a flashlight, a change of clothes, and sturdy shoes by your bed in case the earthquake strikes while you sleep, and you need to evacuate quickly afterward.
2. Keep and maintain a 72-hour emergency kit in an easy-to-access location.
3. Learn how to shut off the gas valves in your home and keep a wrench handy for that purpose. Same thing goes for water valves and electric circuit breakers, if needed
4. Understand that earthquakes also cause fires. Have a fire-evacuation plan as well as an earthquake plan, including escape ladders, etc.
5. Make sure your home is securely anchored to its foundation (mobile homes, etc.).
6. Brace and bolt down water heaters, gas appliances, bookcases, light fixtures, or other furniture to a wall, floor, or ceiling.
7. Place bookshelves or hang heavy items (like pictures and mirrors), away from beds, couches, or anywhere people sit or sleep.
8. Install strong latches or bolts on cabinets. Place large or heavy items close to the floor.
9. Pick a room, hallway, or other location at home, at work, and at school that you can go to if an earthquake begins. Make sure it's away from windows, tall furniture, and other items that may fall on you (e.g., an interior room or under a sturdy table).
10. Practice "drop, cover and hold on" in each safe place you chose above. If you don't have sturdy furniture to hold on to, sit on the floor next to an interior wall (away from windows that might shatter and away from objects that might fall on you) and cover your head and neck with your arms.
11. Study your local public geological records (usually online) to see if you are in a danger zone for "soil liquefaction." Even if you live far away from water, ground water can surface as liquefaction and destroy homes, buildings, and roadways, as well as cut off utility lines causing a shortage of water, electricity, and gas.

DURING AN EARTHQUAKE

If Indoors

1. Stay indoors until shaking stops and it's safe to exit. Stay away from windows.
2. Get under a sturdy table or desk and drop, cover your head and neck, and hold on. If there is nothing to get under, then drop, cover, and move as little as possible.
3. If in bed, stay there, curl up sideways, hold on, and put your pillow over your head and neck for protection.

If Outside

1. If possible and safe to move around, get to a clearing that is away from buildings, landslides, trees, branches, power lines, streetlights, or anything that may fall on you, and then drop to the ground until the shaking stops.
2. If you're driving, pull over to a clear location, away from anything that may fall on you (including landslides or overpasses) and anything that might fall out from under you (like bridges or cliffs), then stop the car, keep your seatbelt on, and wait for the earthquake to end. If a power line falls on your vehicle, don't get out, but wait for assistance. If you need to get out of the vehicle, never touch the floor and the vehicle at the same time, jump from the vehicle with both feet together, and shuffle slowly away.

AFTER AN EARTHQUAKE

1. Expect aftershocks (which may happen several times over minutes or weeks), get yourself to a safe location, and protect yourself each time one happens.
2. Use the stairs, not an elevator, to exit (in case the electricity gets cut off).
3. Use a portable radio (hand-cranked or battery) or smart phones to keep up with the news and listen to the authorities. If they say an area isn't safe, believe them.
4. Check yourself and others around you for injuries and get help if needed.
5. Be aware that the shaking alone may have set off alarms and sprinklers.
6. Extinguish any small fires, and, if safe enough, clean up any small spilt chemical messes, especially flammable or poisonous ones to prevent more problems.
7. Drive carefully. Avoid bridges and ramps that may have been damaged or hillsides that may still produce mud or landslides. Understand that traffic lights may be out.
8. Evacuate homes and locations on the side of a hill that may experience mudslides or landslides.
9. If you are near large bodies of water (even large lakes or rivers), protect yourself against delayed tsunamis or flooding.
10. Watch out for fallen power lines or broken gas lines and stay away from damaged buildings or other unstable locations.
11. Use the telephone only for emergency calls/texts to help cut down on congestion.

PREPARATION EXERCISE

After reading this section, what are some things you would like to do to better prepare yourself, your family, or your group for earthquakes? (write in the section below)

How probable is this crisis a threat to you?
(✔one): □0 □1 □2 □3 □4 □5 □6 □7 □8 □9 □10
How long might this crisis last for you?
(✔one): □3days □3wks □3mos □6mos □1yr □+yrs
Possible nearby threats that concern you:
_____

_____

_____

_____

_____

_____

_____

_____

FIRES (home, forest, grass, car, etc.)
** I recommend you prioritize the study of this section as part of your preparedness. **

On average, a fire is reported in the United States alone every 30-60 seconds with a death resulting every 2-3 hours. Ninety-three percent of emergencies the Red Cross responds to each year are fire related. <u>Fires are the most common emergency, so pay attention!</u>

Fires kill more people each year than ALL other natural disasters combined. With minimal education, most fires can be prevented, and with simple preparations in place, most fire-related deaths would be avoided. Yet, only about 1 in 4 families are prepared for this type of crisis. Let's build some more awareness together.

To better understand this crisis, read the following information compiled from the National Fire Protection Association and the Red Cross:

- The leading causes of fires include kitchen fires, portable heaters, arson, faulty electrical wires, careless smoking, clothes dryers (lint), candles, children playing with fire, Christmas trees, fireworks, chemical/gases, and lightning.
- Cooking-related fires are the leading cause of home fires and cause the most non-fatal injuries (57% start on the stove and 16% start in the oven).
- Even though less than 1% of home-cooking fires started with ignited clothing, these incidents accounted for 15% of cooking-fire deaths.
- Fifty-five percent of people injured in home fires involving cooking equipment were hurt while attempting to fight the fire themselves.
- Failure to clean was a factor contributing to ignition in 17% of reported home fires involving ovens or rotisseries.
- Heater fires (such as portable space heaters or wood stoves) are the second biggest reason for home fires, mainly because they were left too close to upholstered furniture, drapes, clothing, mattresses, or bedding, or they weren't cleaned properly.
- Careless-smoking related fires (cigarettes, etc.) cause the most home-fire deaths. These happen mostly because of alcohol/drug impairment or falling asleep. Twenty-five

percent of the deaths caused by these fires are innocent victims (not the smokers themselves). Over half of the deaths are people over 65 years old and little children.

- Sixty percent of deaths happened in homes that either didn't have fire alarms or the alarms weren't working (battery died or was missing, etc.).
- Half of home fire-related deaths happened between 11:00 p.m. and 7:00 a.m. when most people were sleeping. Only 1 of 5 of these fires actually got reported during those hours. Smoke alarms could have saved these lives.
- Most fires occur during winter months because people are spending more time at home and using more appliances.
- Candle fires happen mostly when a candle is too close to something flammable (like Christmas decorations, drapes, mattresses, etc.) or a person falls asleep with the candle on. Bumping a lit candle or children playing with candles were other reasons.
- The top three days for home candle fires are Christmas Eve, Christmas, and New Year's Day.
- Halogen lights, because of their heat, have a higher risk of fire than incandescent lights, which have a higher risk than fluorescent lights, which have a higher risk than LED lights.
- Though overall more people die from smoking-related fires, hour-for-hour, firework fires cause more deaths than careless smoking overall.
- On Independence Day in a typical year, fireworks account for 2 out of 5 of all reported fires.
- Children under 5 and adults over 65 are more than twice as likely to die in a home fire than the ages in between.
- It can take as little as 30 seconds for a fire to go from inception to out of control.
- Once a fire spreads, temperatures can reach 600°F at eye level which can kill people simply by burning their lungs during inhalation.
- Smoke inhalation injuries (carbon monoxide, etc.), including burns to the respiratory system account for 50–80% of fire-related deaths.

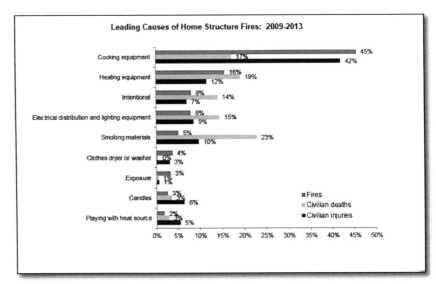

- Fifty percent of all home fires begin in the bedroom, living room, den, or family room.
- High-rise fires are more injurious and cause more damage than all other structure fires.
- Less than half the families that develop a fire safety plan will ever practice it.

PREPARING AND PREVENTING A HOME FIRE – STEPS YOU CAN TAKE NOW

The most effective way to protect yourself and your home from fire is to get educated, identify and remove fire hazards, prepare a plan, and practice it. Let's get started...

Smoke and Carbon Monoxide (CO) Alarms

- Install smoke alarms on every level of your home, inside bedrooms as well as outside sleeping areas. Some alarms even label their products "hallway," "bedroom," "kitchen," and "living area" to help you along.
- Test smoke alarms once a month. If they aren't working, change the batteries. If they still don't work or keep beeping, then replace the alarms.
- It's recommended you replace batteries once a year, and you should replace all of them at the same time, unless you are using an alarm with batteries (like lithium ion) that will last 10 years without replacement.
- Smoke alarms should be replaced about once every 10 years because the sensors get clogged or wear out. You should replace all the alarms in the house at the same time.
- If you move into a pre-owned home (older than 10 years), and you aren't sure if the smoke detectors have been replaced, it's better to be on the safe side and replace them.
- Use a permanent marker to write a "replace by" date on each fire alarm, to take out the guesswork in the future.
- Typically, every 1-3 months, smoke alarm sensors should be cleaned, especially during and after construction or if you live in a dusty location. Follow manufacturer's instructions for cleaning and maintenance. Often, a fast way to clean them is to use a soft-brush attachment and go over the alarm as you vacuum the house.
- Carbon monoxide is an odorless, colorless, deadly, poisonous gas and has been known to be the largest cause of accidental poisoning. It's the silent killer. Install carbon monoxide alarms in central locations, especially near rooms with fireplaces or other gas-burning appliances.
- Teach your children what the different smoke and carbon monoxide alarms sound like and what to do when they hear one.
- Hard-wired smoke alarms work better than simply battery-powered ones. You should use the same brand hard-wired smoke alarms throughout a house to ensure they "talk" to each other properly, so if one goes off, they all do.
- There are 2 types of smoke alarms: ionized and photoelectric. Ionization is the most common (and most sensitive) and responds better to flaming fires, while photoelectric is generally more responsive to smoldering fires. Both may be important depending on your circumstances.
- Test all your alarms as the winter season begins each year, especially before you begin to use candles, space heaters, fireplaces, wood burning stoves, or before putting up your Christmas tree.
- People that are deaf or hard of hearing can purchase special alarms with strobe lights or bed shakers.

In the Kitchen

1. While you're frying, grilling, or broiling food, don't leave the kitchen! When a pan, pot, or deep fryer overheats or splatters grease, fires can ignite in seconds. If you need to leave the kitchen, turn off the stove.
2. Keep combustible materials such as oven mitts, dishtowels, and paper towels, at least 3 feet away from heat sources, and be careful with loose clothing.
3. Keep pets (and children!) off cooking surfaces and countertops to prevent them from injuring themselves and knocking things onto the stove.
4. <u>Don't throw water on a grease fire; it makes it worse</u>! Put a lid on the pan to smother the fire by limiting the oxygen supply. Deep fryers are especially dangerous.
5. Clean leftover debris out of the oven (and stove top) on a regular basis to keep them from scorching and catching fire.
6. If an oven catches fire, immediately close the door (or keep it shut) and turn off the oven so that the fire can extinguish itself from lack of oxygen.
7. Keep a fire extinguisher stored nearby, and make sure everyone knows how to use it. Service or replace your extinguishers on a regular basis as needed.

Careless Smoking

1. If you're going to smoke, smoke outside, and always use wide, deep ashtrays on a sturdy, non-flammable surface (like a table).
2. Never smoke in bed! Don't smoke when you're sleepy, have been drinking, or are taking medicines or drugs that impair your judgment or make you drowsy. If you see someone else starting to fall asleep as they're smoking, take it seriously, and don't let them think that type of careless behavior is okay.
3. Keep lit cigarettes away from medical oxygen units.
4. Since trash fires are some of the biggest culprits, make sure you run a cigarette in water to make sure it's extinguished before you throw out butts and ashes in the trash.
5. Check furniture cushions for fallen cigarettes/embers (a cigarette butt can smolder for hours before causing furniture to burst into flames).

Arson

1. Unfortunately, planned arson is the 3rd most common reason for house fires. What's more dangerous is that 63% of arson happens in structures that are occupied.
2. Arsonists most commonly start their fires in trashcans outside the house, so make sure your trashcans aren't easily accessible.

Electrical & Lighting

1. If you have an older home or apartment, you may have wiring that is worn or inadequate for today's electrical needs. If your lights dim when you use appliances, circuit breakers trip often, or you have to disconnect one appliance to use another, you should have an electrician check your home, just to be safe.
2. Immediately fix frayed wires or loose plugs or sockets.

3. Don't run extension cords or other electrical wires under rugs or furniture.
4. Be careful not to overload home circuitry with too many extension cords plugged into one source. This is one of the bigger reasons for home electrical fires.
5. Christmas lights are essentially "decorated extension cords." Don't leave Christmas lights on overnight or when you leave the home.
6. Keep flammable gases/materials away from electrical sockets where a spark could ignite them.
7. Keep halogen, incandescent, and other light bulbs (that get hot) away from anything that could catch fire.

Children Playing with Fire

1. Children cause fires usually out of curiosity or because they're angry or upset. If you find matches or lighters, either hidden or in their possession, or if you find their toys or furniture with burn marks, talk to your children about fire safety and set some rules.
2. Children under the age of 6 typically start fires indoors (usually in bedrooms) and older children usually start fires outside. Boys, rather than girls, start 83% of these fires, and July is the most active month.
3. From a young age, talk to your children regularly about the dangers of fire, including matches and lighters, and keep them out of reach, if needed.

Fireplaces & Barbecues

1. Chimneys sometimes get backed-up and need occasional cleaning. Especially if you burn wood in your fireplace, a buildup of soot or creosote 1/8th inch thick or more in your chimney is a dangerous candidate for fire threats. Fireplaces are built to withstand the heat of fire, but chimneys typically are not. If a fire catches inside the chimney, the lining can crack, and flames can reach the home or building's structure. Fire and sparks can also spew out the top of the chimney, causing the roof to ignite.
2. If you burn wood or use your fireplace often, get it checked or cleaned yearly. Chimney sweepers could be "good luck" in these circumstances.
3. Install a carbon monoxide alarm nearby rooms with fireplaces to alert you of deadly carbon monoxide gas.
4. Equip chimneys and stovepipes with spark arresters.
5. Never use a grill, BBQ, camp stove or other gasoline, propane, natural gas, or charcoal-burning device indoors (including garages) because of ignition blasts, sparks, or unexpected fires. Burning anything with an open flame puts off carbon monoxide, which can be deadly, especially indoors or other enclosed spaces.
6. Regularly clean barbecues and their removable parts (inside and out) with soapy water to keep food scraps and grease from building up and becoming potential fire hazards.
7. Occasionally spray barbeque gas/propane connectors, pipes, or nozzles with soapy water to make sure there aren't any gas leaks. Watch if bubbles form when you open the gas. If they do, turn them off, and get them repaired immediately.
8. Use barbecues away from your home, deck rails, loose clothing, tablecloths, tree limbs, or anything combustible. Be especially careful when igniting the barbecue.

Portable Heaters

1. Test your fire alarms before starting to use your portable heaters for the season.
2. Keep items that can catch on fire (including bedding, drapes, deep-pile carpet, and clothes) at least 3-5 feet away from space heaters.
3. Avoid using extension cords with portable heaters because of the amount of power they draw.
4. Never use your heaters to dry shoes or clothes.
5. Turn portable heaters off when you leave the room or go to sleep.

Candles

1. Never leave a burning candle unattended. Blow out candles when you leave a room or when you go to sleep.
2. Keep children and pets away from lit candles.
3. Keep candles at least 3-5 feet away from anything combustible like Christmas trees, presents, decorations, artwork, bedding, clothes, drapes, or wooden objects.
4. Use candles in very sturdy candleholders or in enclosed containers (like glass jars) and place them on sturdy surfaces.

Christmas Trees/Decorations

1. The combination of a dry tree with gifts underneath (as a fuel source), keeps firemen quite busy in December and early January every year. Take some precautions, and keep your trees away from all heat sources, including fireplaces, wood stoves, candles, radiators, portable heaters, furnace ducts, etc.
2. If you have a "real" Christmas tree, keep the tree in a stand that will hold at least 2 liters of water in it. Top it off daily to keep the tree alive and green as long as possible.
3. Dispose of Christmas trees before they get dry.
4. Check decorative lights before placing them on the tree, and discard or repair any frayed, damaged, or shorted cords/lights.
5. Turn off Christmas lights before going to bed or leaving the house.

Clothes Dryers

1. Clothes-dryer fires happen more often than you think, causing about $200 million in property damage each year, according to the NFPA. It happens mostly when lint ignites from the surrounding heat or from electrical sparks. The risk of fire is basically the same for both gas and electric-powered dryers.
2. Since it's so flammable, regularly clean out lint in, around, and under the dryer, as well as in the ducts.
3. Never run a dryer without the lint screen in place.
4. Occasionally vacuum <u>and</u> wash the lint collector since dryer sheets can leave a film on the collector and prevent proper airflow.

5. Ensure the dryer vent in back doesn't get smashed or pinched when moving the dryer around. The drying vent should have a clear pathway to the outside of the house.
6. For propane or gas dryers, make sure there aren't any leaks in the gas lines.
7. Keep the area around the dryer free from combustible materials.
8. Set a timer to not let your clothes over dry.

Flammables In/Around the House

1. Store flammable liquids (such as thinners, solvents, cleaning agents, adhesives, paints, and other flammable raw materials) in secure, proper containers. Store them at least 10 feet away from any spark or fire source.
2. Keep flammable materials out of direct sunlight or other places where high temperatures can cause vapors to ignite spontaneously.

Lightning

1. Unlike other types of house fires, which usually occur in the winter, lightning fires occur more often in the dry/hot months of summer, especially in the late afternoon.
2. If you live near a forest or wooded area, make sure there is enough of a clearing between the woods and your house, and make sure dry grass or similar foliage is kept short in nearby fields.

BEFORE A FIRE

1. Implement ideas from the sections above and create a good fire-emergency plan.
2. Make sure every person in your family or group knows at least 2 ways to escape a fire from each location in your house or building.
3. Have a designated place to meet outside to make sure everyone makes it out safely.
4. Practice 1-2 times a year different scenarios such as low-crawling to avoid smoke and heat, touching a closed door to see if it's hot (a sign of a fire on the other side), meeting outside, using an escape ladder, what to do if you're sleeping in bed when an alarm goes off, etc. Practice helps reduce anxieties and life-threatening mistakes that might happen in the "heat" of the actual crisis.
5. Purchase small bats or other tools for breaking windows during a fire in order to escape and put one in each bedroom or office. You can also add a towel (or leather piece) that can be used to drape over a windowsill to avoid being cut as you get out.
6. Put a whistle in each room so people can alert others that they are still inside.
7. Put a flashlight in each room in case the electricity fails. This can also be used to signal others from a window that you are still in the house/building.
8. For second stories, buy compact ladders made for fire escape and put one in each bedroom at home or each office space at work.
9. Consider purchasing a fireproof safe for valuables and documents.
10. Make sure your house number and/or address is clearly marked on the house and on the curb for firemen to easily locate.

11. Create a "defensible space" by surrounding your house with plants, trees, and materials that resist fire. Also, clear away plants, trees, and materials that pose potential dangers (e.g., hardwood trees are less flammable than evergreen or pine trees). Keep firewood at least 30 feet from the house.
12. Regularly clear away your air conditioner, roof, and rain gutters of dried leaves and debris.
13. For wildfires, know sources of water near your home you can use (e.g. swimming pools, ponds, wells, etc.) and have tools (e.g. shovel, ax, chain saw, rake, bucket, gloves, and sturdy shoes) to help fight off small fires, if necessary, until fire professionals arrive.
14. Install fire-resistant siding, roofing, and other building materials.
15. Video (or take pictures) of your home and your belongings in each room and make a list of valuable items (for insurance purposes). Store these pictures or videos and any important documents in a safe place (e.g., fireproof safe or online cloud storage).

DURING A FIRE

1. Follow your fire escape plan and remember to GET OUT (and get to your designated meeting place), STAY OUT, and *then* CALL 9-1-1. Always remember the rule, "if in doubt, get out!"
2. Remember to use your 2 (or more) ways to escape (including ladders for 2nd or 3rd story escapes).
3. If your clothes are on fire, remember to STOP, DROP and ROLL.
4. Get low and crawl under smoke, where needed and where possible.
5. If closed doors or door handles are warm, use your second way out. Never open doors that are warm to the touch.
6. If all your escape routes are blocked with smoke or flames, stay in the room with doors closed and put a wet towel (or something that won't catch fire easily) under the door to keep the smoke from coming in. If you can, open a window and use a whistle, wave your hands or a bright cloth, or use a flashlight or mirror to signal to others that you're still inside. Stay by opened windows to avoid carbon monoxide inhalation, if possible.
7. If the fire is small, the room is not filled with smoke, and you know the fire can be put out easily and effectively, then extinguish it safely.
8. If you have/use a traditional fire extinguisher, remember the PASS method:
   o **P** – Pull the pin and hold the extinguisher with the nozzle pointing away from you.
   o **A** – Aim low. Point the extinguisher at the base of the fire.
   o **S** – Squeeze the lever slowly and evenly.
   o **S** – Sweep the nozzle from side to side.

For wildfires, tune into local radio or television stations. Keep your doors and windows closed to limit smoke inhalation. If needed, get ready to evacuate at a moment's notice (load your car with needed items and park it ready for escape) and arrange temporary housing outside of the danger area.

AFTER A FIRE

1. Check yourself and others for injuries and get help if needed.
2. Stay out of a home or building until it's completely safe to go in.
3. Once you go back to a damaged structure, wear as many protective items as you can to avoid injuries (e.g. long pants, long sleeve shirt or coat, sturdy boots with rubber soles, hat or helmet, work gloves, mask to not breath in poisons, goggles, etc.).
4. Only after the authorities give you the okay, salvage important documents and items where possible.
5. Wet down debris to avoid breathing in dust and ash particles and to extinguish any hot spots or embers.
6. Take several pictures and notify your insurance company of the fire. Keep receipts of all your expenses related to the fire (such as temporary housing, clothes, etc.)
7. Avoid damaged or exposed electrical cords, power lines, or harmful chemicals/debris.
8. Dispose of food that has been exposed to heat, smoke, and ash, and be careful of using or drinking contaminated water (even if water looks clear, it may be contaminated).

PREPARATION EXERCISE

After reading this section, what are some things you would like to do to better prepare yourself, your family, or your group for fire hazards? (write in the section below)

How probable is this crisis a threat to you?
(✔one): □0 □1 □2 □3 □4 □5 □6 □7 □8 □9 □10
How long might this crisis last for you?
(✔one): □3days □3wks □3mos □6mos □1yr □+yrs
Possible nearby threats that concern you:
_____

_____

_____

_____

_____

_____

_____

_____

_____

Hurricanes, Typhoons, Cyclones

Hurricanes, Typhoons, and Cyclones are <u>the same thing</u>, people just call them by different names in different parts of the world ("Hurricanes" in the Atlantic and Central & Eastern North Pacific Ocean, "Typhoons" in the Northwest Pacific Ocean, and "Cyclones" in the Indian and South Pacific Oceans). The scientific name for these 3 is "Tropical Cyclones."

Tropical cyclones are large-scale rotating storm systems that can have horizontal dimensions from 60 miles (97 km) to over 1300 miles (2092 km) in diameter (very different from tornadoes that only get about 2.5 miles in diameter, at the very most).

Hurricanes form in the ocean, and never form at the equator (because of the Coriolis force), but often originate in tropical zones between 5 and 20-degrees latitude. Using warm surface water temperatures above 76°F (25°C) to draw their strength, hurricanes can travel thousands of miles, persist for days, and create havoc, especially as they approach land.

In North America, tropical cyclone (hurricane) season begins near June 1st and ends around November 30th each year. When they do happen, cyclones are categorized 1-5 by wind speed in miles per hour, 1 being "minimal" and 5 being "catastrophic."

HURRICANE CATEGORIES		
CATEGORY	WIND	DAMAGE
1	74-95	Minimal
2	96-110	Moderate
3	111-130	Extensive
4	131-155	Extreme
5	156 or more	Catastrophic

If you live near the coast, you may want to learn about the history of tropical cyclones (hurricanes, typhoons, cyclones) in your area by doing a simple Internet search.

BEFORE A TROPICAL CYCLONE (HURRICANE)

1. Fill up your car(s) with gasoline (a great practice to prepare for any emergency situation), in case of evacuation or post-crisis gasoline shortages.
2. Have 72-hour emergency supplies ready to "grab and go" if needed.
3. Take inventory of any power lines or large trees that may pose a threat to your home or work locations during high winds. Trim back or remove trees that may fall or lose large branches and damage your home.
4. Install hurricane shutters, reinforced garage doors, and hurricane straps for the roof.
5. Protect your home and basement against possible flooding (see the flooding section).
6. Create a hurricane evacuation plan. Get to hurricane shelters, where possible, or other locations that won't flood or be damaged by wind. If stuck at home, get yourself to the most secure and safe room in the house, away from the windows that might shatter.
7. Be prepared to last weeks without public utilities, shopping, etc.

DURING A TROPICAL CYCLONE (HURRICANE)

1. Turn the radio and television on for the latest news.
2. Bring inside anything you don't want swept away, such as lawn furniture, trash cans, toys, bikes, tools, etc.
3. Put your cars in the garage to avoid debris crashing into them.
4. Close your doors and hurricane shutters or board up the windows and doors with plywood (not particle board or other unsuitable materials).
5. Unplug small appliances and turn off propane and other utilities as needed.
6. Get to your places of safety.
7. Evacuate quickly if authorities say to do so. Shut off gas, water, and electricity before you leave, if there's time.

AFTER A TROPICAL CYCLONE (HURRICANE)

1. Keep tuned into the news.
2. Stay away from flooded or damaged buildings because they may be unstable.
3. Avoid loose or damaged power lines.
4. Understand that flooded areas may contain water that is contaminated with sewage, gasoline, or other harmful chemicals.
5. If there is a threat of gas leaks, use flashlights instead of candles or flames of any sort.
6. If the electricity is down, keep the refrigerator closed as much as possible to keep the cold in and preserve your food or move your refrigerated food to a high-quality cooler.
7. Before you drink from tap water, make sure it isn't contaminated.
8. If you need to evacuate, only return when the authorities say it is safe to do so.

PREPARATION EXERCISE

After reading this section, what are some things you would like to do to better prepare yourself, your family, or your group for hurricanes, typhoons, cyclones?
(write in the section below)

> **How probable is this crisis a threat to you?**
> (✔one): □0 □1 □2 □3 □4 □5 □6 □7 □8 □9 □10
> **How long might this crisis last for you?**
> (✔one): □3days □3wks □3mos □6mos □1yr □+yrs
> **Possible nearby threats that concern you:**
> _____

_____

_____

_____

_____

_____

Tornadoes (or Other High Winds)

Tornadoes and hurricanes appear to be similar in their general structure because of extremely strong horizontal winds swirling around and around, but, in reality, they're very different.

Where hurricanes can last for days and can be 1000 miles in diameter, tornadoes typically last from only a few minutes up to a few hours and don't get much bigger than a couple miles wide, at the most. Where hurricanes often give you plenty of warning, tornadoes don't.

Compared to hurricanes, tornadoes are considered "small-scale circulations." But, don't let the "small" make you under-estimate their destructive force.

The Enhanced Fujita Scale	
EF Rating	3 second gust (mph)
0	65-85
1	86-110
2	111-135
3	136-165
4	166-200
5	over 200

Like hurricanes, tornadoes range from minimal (EF-0) to "catastrophic" (EF-5). At EF-0, you can expect to lose shingles, a few branches, and see shallow-rooted trees toppled. At EF-5, you can expect to see well-constructed homes swept away, trees completely debarked, and steel or concrete structures critically damaged.

In North America, tornado season is typically between the months of April through June as the surrounding land heats up.

MORE INTERESTING TORNADO FACTS

The Deadliest Tornado happened in the Manikganj District of Bangladesh on April 26, 1989. An estimated 1300 people died as the 1-mile wide tornado traveled about 50 miles through many poor areas and slums. About 12,000 people were injured and about 80,000 left homeless. A local newspaper wrote, "The devastation was so complete, that barring some skeletons of trees, there were no signs of standing structures."

The widest tornado ever recorded hit El Reno, Oklahoma on May 31ˢᵗ, 2013. It was 2.6 miles wide and rated EF-5. Wind speeds hit over 295 mph, and traveling over 16 miles, it lasted for about 40 minutes.

Luckily it missed the heavily populated metropolitan areas, yet there were 8 fatalities (including 4 storm chasers), 151 people injured, and about $40 million in damages.

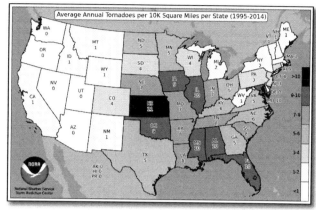

The longest tornado track-of-damage is the infamous "Tri-State Tornado." It touched down on March 18, 1925 and cut across the Upper Mississippi Valley hitting Missouri, Illinois, and Indiana over a 3.5-hour period. It traveled 235 miles, killing 695 people and injuring over 2000 more.

Signs of a Tornado

Since tornadoes offer little advanced notice, keep your radios and televisions set to the local news, and pay attention to the following signs:

1. Look for strong, persistent rotations in the cloud base.
2. Be aware of whirling dust or debris on the ground under a cloud base (tornadoes sometimes have no funnel).
3. Listen for hail or heavy rain followed by either dead calm or a fast, intense wind shift. Many tornadoes are wrapped in heavy precipitation and can't be seen.
4. Pay attention to loud, continuous roars or rumbles, which don't fade in a few seconds like thunder does.
5. At night, look for small, bright, blue-green or white flashes at ground level near a thunderstorm (as opposed to silvery lightning up in the clouds). These mean power lines are being snapped by very strong winds, maybe even a tornado. Also, be aware of a potential tornado if you see clouds persistently lowering. You can use lightning flashes to gauge their location, if needed.

BEFORE A TORNADO

1. Keep your car fuel tank at least half full at all times (a great practice to prepare for any emergency situation), in case of evacuation.
2. Have 72-hour emergency supplies ready to "grab and go" if needed.
3. Take inventory of any power lines or large trees that may pose a threat to your home or work locations during high winds. Trim back or remove trees that may fall or damage your home with loose large branches.
4. Determine the safest room (or location) to be in during a tornado (at home, work, or at school).
5. Install a storm shelter and register it so people can look for you there.
6. Create an emergency tornado plan (including an evacuation plan) and practice it.
7. Reinforce the windows, doors, garage door, roof, and chimney of your house.

DURING A POSSIBLE TORNADO THREAT

1. Turn the radio and television on for the latest news.
2. If there's time, bring inside anything that's outside you don't want swept away, like lawn furniture, trash cans, toys, bikes, tools, etc. These may also become projected missiles during high winds and hurt people or damage property.
3. If there's time, put your cars in the garage to avoid debris crashing into them.
4. Unplug small appliances, since they may be damaged by power surges.
5. Turn off propane tanks in case they are damaged or dislodged by strong winds or water. Shutting them off can help prevent fires from starting.
6. Turn off other utilities, if needed, especially if requested by authorities to do so.
7. Evacuate quickly if authorities say to do so.
8. Be aware of flying debris (including large hail) – REMEMBER, flying debris are the most common cause of deaths and injuries during tornadoes.
9. **If you're caught in a <u>house</u>.** Avoid windows! Move to a sheltered location such as a storm shelter, a basement or a small interior room or hallway on the lowest floor and get under a sturdy piece of furniture (heavy table or workbench) or in a bathtub. Put as many walls as possible between you and the outside, and make sure there are no heavy objects (like a refrigerator or piano) right above you in case they fall down through a weakened floor. Wear a helmet and cover yourself with a mattress, sleeping bag, or heavy blankets, if possible.
10. **If you're caught in a <u>building</u>.** Go to the lowest floor and stay toward the center of the building, under a stairwell, in a bathroom, or a hallway away from all windows. Crouch as low as possible to the floor, facing down; and cover your head/neck with your hands. Stay off the elevators because you could be trapped in them if the power is lost.
11. **If you're caught in a <u>mobile home</u>.** Get out! Even if your home is tied down, it's not safe. Get to an underground shelter or a permanent, sturdy building or home and follow the advice above.
12. **If you're caught in a <u>vehicle</u>.** Vehicles are extremely risky in a tornado. There's no safe option when caught in a car during a tornado, just slightly less-dangerous ones. If the tornado is visible, far enough away, and the traffic is light, you may be able to drive out of its way by moving perpendicular to its path and, if there's time, seek shelter in a sturdy building or underground location. If you're caught in extreme winds or flying debris, park the car as quickly and safely as possible, out of the traffic lanes. Avoid seeking shelter under bridges (which can create deadly traffic hazards while offering little protection against flying debris). Stay in the car with the seat belt on and put your head down below the windows in case objects fly through them. Cover your head with your hands, a blanket, coat, or other cushion, if possible. If you can safely get noticeably lower than the level of the roadway (like a deep ditch or depression), leave your car and lie in that area, covering your head with your hands.
13. **If you're caught <u>outdoors</u>.** If possible, seek shelter in a sturdy building. If you can't get to one, lie as flat as you can, facedown, low to the ground, protecting the back of your head with your arms. If you can find a hole, deep ditch, or depression, get in that instead and lay down. Stay as far away from trees, electric poles, and cars as you can since they may be blown on top of you during the tornado.

AFTER A TORNADO

1. Check yourself and others for injuries and get help if needed.
2. Keep tuned into the news just in case there are threats of more tornadoes coming.
3. Avoid loose or damaged power lines.
4. If there is a threat of gas leaks, use flashlights instead of candles or flames of any sort.
5. If the electricity is down, keep the refrigerator closed as much as possible to keep the cold in and preserve your food or move your refrigerated food to a high-quality cooler.
6. Before you drink from tap water, make sure it isn't contaminated.
7. If you needed to evacuate, only return when the authorities say it is safe to do so.

PREPARATION EXERCISE

After reading this section, what are some things you would like to do to better prepare yourself, your family, or your group for tornadoes? (write in the section below)

How probable is this crisis a threat to you?
(✔one): □0 □1 □2 □3 □4 □5 □6 □7 □8 □9 □10
How long might this crisis last for you?
(✔one): □3days □3wks □3mos □6mos □1yr □+yrs
Possible nearby threats that concern you:
_____

_____

_____

_____

_____

_____

_____

_____

_____

_____

_____

_____

Floods

Every country around the world, and every part of the United States, faces the threat of flooding to some degree. Flooding happens for several reasons, including:

- Ice/Snow Melt Flooding
- Large Rainstorms
- River/Lake Overflows
- Flash Floods
- Runoff
- Hurricanes
- Tsunamis or Rogue Waves
- Dam Ruptures
- Canal, Pipe, or Water-Main Ruptures
- Soil Liquefaction (where soil becomes a fluid-like mass during or after an earthquake)

Consider where you live or work carefully. Are there any possible flooding threats you may face in the future? If so, how severe can they become, and what can you do to ensure your safety and the safety of your irreplaceable keepsakes? Do you have an evacuation route? Where would you relocate?

The damage that floods cause can be extensive. Floods can damage bridges, roads, railways, and even entire towns. Buildings, cars, and houses can be left saturated or completely taken away by the waters.

Power grids, gas lines, and water mains can be destroyed, leaving residents without utilities or clean drinking water for weeks. After the floodwaters recede, lands can be contaminated with hazardous materials, such as toxic chemicals, fuel, and untreated sewage. All this can lead to deadly disease outbreaks.

BEFORE A FLOOD

1. Avoid living in a floodplain unless you elevate and reinforce your home or building.
2. Elevate the furnace, water heater, and electric panel if susceptible to flooding.
3. Install "check valves" in sewer traps to prevent floodwater from backing up into the drains of your home.
4. Construct barriers (levees, berms, floodwalls) to stop floodwaters from entering your house or building.
5. Move/Store Important Keepsakes on Higher Levels

6. Seal walls in basements with waterproofing compounds to avoid seepage.
7. Prepare a 72-hour survival kit in the case of sudden evacuation.

DURING FLOODING THREATS

1. Listen to the radio or television for information.
2. Be aware that flash flooding can occur. If there is any possibility of a flash flood, move immediately to higher ground. Don't wait for instructions to move.
3. Be aware of streams, drainage channels, canyons, and other areas known to flood suddenly. Flash floods can occur in these areas with or without typical warnings such as rain clouds or heavy rain.
4. Stay out of valleys or canyons and away from rivers and streams, including overpasses.
5. Be careful of mud/landslides if you live on or near a hill, cliff, or other incline.

Evacuation Procedures

1. Secure your home. If you have time, bring in outdoor furniture and other things you might lose in the flood. Move essential items and keepsakes to an upper floor.
2. <u>Don't touch electrical items if you're wet or standing in water</u>. If it's safe to do so, shut off utilities at the main switches or valves and disconnect electrical appliances.
3. Don't walk through moving water. Six inches of moving water can make you fall. If you have to walk in water, walk where the water is not moving. Use a stick to check the firmness of the ground or the depth of the water in front of you.
4. Don't drive into flooded areas. If floodwaters rise around your car, and you can do so safely, abandon the car and move to higher ground. As little as a foot of water can float a vehicle (causing stalling and loss of control), and two feet of rushing water can carry away most vehicles including sport utility vehicles (SUV's) and pick-ups.

AFTER A FLOOD

1. Listen for news reports to learn whether the community's water supply is safe to drink.
2. Avoid getting wet by the floodwaters since oil, gasoline, raw sewage, or other chemicals may have contaminated the water. Water may also be electrically charged from underground or downed power lines as well.
3. Avoid moving waters. Even slow-moving water may be more powerful than you think.
4. Be aware of areas where floodwaters have receded. Roads may have weakened and could collapse under the weight of a car.
5. Clean and disinfect everything that got wet. Mud left from floodwater can contain chemicals, sewage, and harmful microbes.
6. Stay away from downed power lines and report them to the power company ASAP.
7. If you needed to evacuate, return home only when authorities indicate it's safe.
8. Use extreme caution when entering buildings near or in the flooded areas because of possible hidden damage, particularly in foundations.
9. Service damaged septic tanks or cesspools as soon as possible. Damaged sewage systems are serious health hazards.

PREPARATION EXERCISE

After reading this section, what are some things you would like to do to better prepare yourself, your family, or your group for flooding? (write in the section below)

How probable is this crisis a threat to you?
(✔one): □0 □1 □2 □3 □4 □5 □6 □7 □8 □9 □10
How long might this crisis last for you?
(✔one): □3days □3wks □3mos □6mos □1yr □+yrs
Possible nearby threats that concern you:
_____

_____

_____

_____

_____

_____

_____

_____

_____

_____

_____

_____

_____

_____

_____

_____

_____

_____

_____

Droughts

Did you know that the average American uses about 80-100 gallons (379 liters) of water a day!? Do you know how much you use a day? What if you were forced to reduce your use to 50 or 10 or 2 gallons (7.5 liters) per day for months on end? How would you survive?

In the U.S., if you live in California, Nevada, Oregon, Utah, Arizona, Idaho, Washington, New Mexico, South Dakota, Kansas, Texas, Colorado, or Oklahoma, you're more familiar with drought warnings, yet none of the United States is completely exempt. Droughts occur in virtually every climate.

A drought is defined as a period of abnormally dry weather that persists long enough to produce serious damages to the environment, the economy, or life itself. For example, droughts can cause crop damage, death of livestock, and even reduced output from hydroelectric plants which can limit your electric use. Droughts can also cause large businesses to be scaled back, sold off, or shut down. Small towns may be abandoned as running water disappears.

According to the National Climate Data Center, droughts cause more economic damage in the U.S. than any other natural disaster, except for hurricanes.

Drought Severity Classification

Category	Description	Possible Impacts
D0	Abnormally Dry	Going into drought: • short-term dryness slowing planting, growth of crops or pastures Coming out of drought: • some lingering water deficits • pastures or crops not fully recovered
D1	Moderate Drought	• Some damage to crops, pastures • Streams, reservoirs, or wells low, some water shortages developing or imminent • Voluntary water-use restrictions requested
D2	Severe Drought	• Crop or pasture losses likely • Water shortages common • Water restrictions imposed
D3	Extreme Drought	• Major crop/pasture losses • Widespread water shortages or restrictions
D4	Exceptional Drought	• Exceptional and widespread crop/pasture losses • Shortages of water in reservoirs, streams, and wells creating water emergencies

Short-term droughts typically last less than 6 months and long-term more than 6 months. The level of drought "severity" is measured from D-0 (abnormally dry) to D-4 (life-threatening or "exceptional").

BEFORE A DROUGHT

1. Follow PrepSteps #2-7 in this course to make sure you have enough water, food, supplies, and savings to endure a drought crisis for at least 6-12 months.

DURING A DROUGHT

1. Keep storing water and other life-saving supplies, if possible
2. Follow the water restrictions your state or city officials recommend.
3. Try to do at least one little thing extra each day to conserve water.
4. Try washing cars at night to avoid evaporation. In fact, you could wash your car on top of the grass and double up! Also, use buckets to wash cars and a nozzle on the hose to shut off the water when you aren't using it. Patronize car washes that recycle their water.
5. Never pour wastewater down the drain when there may be another use for it. For example, capture cold water as you wait for it to turn warm and then use it to water your plants or wash your car.
6. Make sure your home is leak-free, including toilets and well pumps. You can test your toilet by putting a couple drops of food coloring in the tank and see if it is leaking into the bowl. One drop of water leaked every second wastes about 416 gallons per year!
7. Toilets are one of the biggest water wasters. Flush your toilet less often (or install water conserving toilets), and if you're brave enough, you can follow the rule "if it's yellow, leave it mellow, but if it's brown, then flush it down." Trees in your back yard are also an option, but your neighbors might not approve. ☺
8. Don't leave the water running while shaving, brushing your teeth, washing your face, or lathering up in the shower. Get wet, turn the water off, lather up, then turn the water back on to rinse off.
9. Replace old showerheads with low-flow heads or put a bucket in the shower to catch excess water (to water plants, etc.).
10. Purchase water-efficient dishwashers, clothes washers, etc.
11. Run your dishwasher only after it's full or wash dishes by hand by filling up 2 sinks or containers – one with soapy water and the other with clean water. You can add in a few drops of chlorine in the water to help with sanitation.
12. Create a compost pile rather than running water to use the garbage disposal.
13. Thaw meats overnight in the refrigerator or on the "defrost" setting in the microwave, not under running water.
14. Wash full loads of clothes at a time, or if you have smaller loads, use the setting that's right for the amount of clothes you're washing (small, medium, large, or extra-large load).
15. Cover pools and Jacuzzis (hot tubs) to reduce evaporation.
16. Replace landscaping with decorative rocks and plants that require very little water. Often, native plants and drought-resistant grasses, shrubs, and trees will survive a dry period much longer without watering.
17. Add peat moss to your garden soil and cover flowerbeds with bark or another ground covering that helps retain moisture and requires less frequent watering.
18. Use drip irrigation systems on plants rather than a hose. A running hose can waste 50 gallons of water every 10 minutes.

19. Don't overwater lawns. Water in small spurts so water has time to penetrate the ground. Water in the evening or night to reduce evaporation. Turn off automatic sprinklers during heavy rains and keep them off until several days afterward, if the ground is well soaked. If rains can fill up an empty tuna can you place outside, then you probably have enough water in the ground to last nearly a week (in most areas) without re-watering the grass.
20. Make sure your sprinklers are actually watering the plants, not the sidewalk.
21. Mow your lawn at the tallest grass setting. Your grass will grow back slower as the roots grow deeper, and the extra shade will conserve more water.

AFTER A DROUGHT

1. Follow PrepSteps #2-7 in this course to replenish your supplies for future emergency situations.

PREPARATION EXERCISE

After reading this section, what are some things you would like to do to better prepare yourself, your family, or your group for droughts?
(write in the section below)

> **How probable is this crisis a threat to you?**
> (✔one): □0 □1 □2 □3 □4 □5 □6 □7 □8 □9 □10
> **How long might this crisis last for you?**
> (✔one): □3days □3wks □3mos □6mos □1yr □+yrs
> **Possible nearby threats that concern you:**
> _____

_____

_____

_____

_____

_____

_____

_____

_____

_____

Heat Waves

Most people don't know this, but heat waves are the most lethal type of any "weather-related" phenomenon, even more than other natural disasters such as floods, lightning, tornadoes, and hurricanes. For example, in less than a week, over 700 people died in the 1995 Chicago heat wave. More than 70,000 people died in the horrors of the 2003 European heat wave. In the 2010 Russian heat wave, upwards of 55,000 died. Each year, there are thousands of tragedies around the world, simply because people aren't prepared for heat waves.

A heat wave occurs when there is a prolonged period of excessive heat that is usually 10 degrees or more above average. When combined with excessive humidity, heat waves can become even deadlier and more destructive.

Severe heat waves can cause catastrophic crop failures, wildfires, and physical damage to roads and highways that buckle and crack. People get stressed, thinking gets impaired, and crime levels (even murder) increase. Water lines can burst, power transformers can overload and catch fire, and power outages take place since too many air-conditioners are running at the same time, etc.

Besides the hundreds of deaths each year in the U.S. alone, the Agency for Health Care Research and Quality claims that about 6,200 Americans are hospitalized each summer due to excessive heat. Those at highest risk are the poor, the uninsured, or the elderly. The death toll increases considerably after 65 years of age and spikes up tremendously after 75.

Other at-risk groups include little children under 4 years old, sick or overweight individuals, pregnant mothers, and chronically-ill people taking medications that keep their bodies from dissipating heat effectively.

Heat waves are measured by the heat index (see the accompanying chart).

The heat index doesn't measure simply how hot it is, but it measures how hot the day *feels*. For

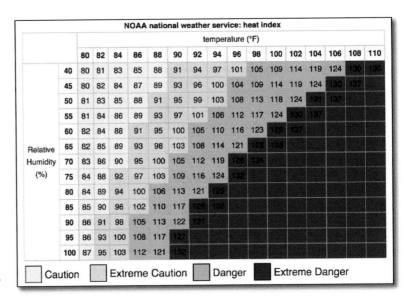

34

example, it may only be 88°F (31°C) outside, but at 80% humidity, it *feels* like 106°F (41°C). Or, it may be 90°F (32°C), but at 95% humidity, it *feels* like 127°F (53°C), and that puts you in the extreme danger category.

Excessive heat poses a number of health risks, which include:

Heat Edema – A swelling of the hands, feet, and ankles due to water retention.

Heat Rash (also known as "Prickly Heat") – A rash that happens mostly to areas of the body covered by tight clothing. The sweat ducts may dilate and eventually rupture and may lead to bacterial infections.

Heat Cramps – Painful involuntary spasms in large muscle groups typically during exercise or sports when heavy sweating isn't replenished with enough electrolytes (from sport drinks, etc.).

Heat Exhaustion (also known as "Heat Prostration" or "Heat Stress") – The forerunner to Heat Stroke. Heat exhaustion is marked by excessive dehydration and electrolyte depletion followed by symptoms such as heavy breathing, a fast and weak pulse, low blood pressure, diarrhea, nausea, dizziness, headaches, vomiting, etc.

Heat Stroke (also known as "Hyperthermia") – The body loses its ability to cool itself and begins to shut down. This may result in all the symptoms of heat exhaustion coupled with other symptoms such as seizures and impaired thinking (e.g. a confused, hostile, or seemingly intoxicated behavior). If not caught in time and reversed, eventually the result will be organ failure, unconsciousness, and death.

BEFORE A HEAT WAVE

1. Take time to understand the dangers of heat waves (above) and take time to insulate your home, install cooling systems, and/or create good heat wave emergency plans.
2. Understand the difference between outside temperature and the heat index.

DURING A HEAT WAVE

1. Pay attention to the "feels like" portion of the news or weather-related websites.
2. Never leave a child or pet in a car when there is hot weather to any degree. If pets are outside, give them access to a shaded area and plenty of water. Check on them frequently.
3. Even if you (and others around you) don't feel thirsty, stay extra hydrated, drink electrolytes (e.g. sport drinks), and replenish your body with some salts (snacks, etc.). Avoid drinks with caffeine or alcohol in them.
4. Eat smaller meals and eat meals more often.
5. If you don't have air conditioning, find a public building such as a mall, school, library, restaurant, or theater you can go to for relief during the hottest parts of the day of a heat wave.

6. It's better to wear lightweight, light-colored, loose-fitting clothing in the heat to avoid heat rash. Remember, white (or lighter colors) reflects heat, and black (or darker colors) absorbs heat.

7. Postpone or avoid strenuous exercise, outdoor games, or other activities during the hottest part of the day.

8. Slow down and avoid extreme temperature changes between hot and cold.

9. During heat waves, take extra precautions if you're in a city or suburb. Physical structures (such as buildings and roads) can absorb and retain heat creating an "urban heat island" that can actually be much hotter than what's reported in the news.

10. If you work outside, take extra breaks, and use a buddy system to check on each other.

11. Be aware of the very young, old, sick, overweight, and pregnant around you. Also, take note of persons without air conditioning (especially if they live alone), and help them take extra precautions.

12. Recognize signs of heat exhaustion, including cool, moist, pale, or flushed skin, headaches, weakness, weak or fast-paced heartbeats, dizziness, nausea, or exhaustion. These are all precursors to heat stroke and may result in death. If concerned, get the person into a cooler environment with circulating air, loosen or remove unneeded clothing, and get them into a comfortable position and relaxed. Also, put wet and cool towels on their skin (or maybe even ice packs), spray water on their face, neck, wrists, and ankles, use a fan, and have them drink cool sport drinks (with electrolytes) and not *just* water (4 ounces of liquid every 15 minutes). Avoid giving them straight salts (no salt pills). If they feel comfortable enough to do so, they can take a cool shower or bath in between being replenished with electrolytes.

13. If the person is acting erratically and refusing to drink liquids or get help, or if there are more severe symptoms such as losing consciousness, vomiting, seizures, discolored skin, and high body temperatures, then heat stroke may be settling in. Call 9-1-1 and get immediate professional help.

PREPARATION EXERCISE

After reading this section, what are some things you would like to do to better prepare yourself, your family, or your group for heat waves? (write in the section below)

How probable is this crisis a threat to you?
(✓one): □0 □1 □2 □3 □4 □5 □6 □7 □8 □9 □10
How long might this crisis last for you?
(✓one): □3days □3wks □3mos □6mos □1yr □+yrs
Possible nearby threats that concern you:
_____

_____

_____

_____

_____

Cold Waves

Specific to each geographic location (and time of year), a cold wave is a rapid fall in temperature within a 24-hour period that substantially threatens agriculture, industry, commerce, social activities, and life itself. It varies for each location.

For example, typical freezing winter temperatures in Alaska, Minnesota, Winnipeg, Siberia, or Finland, might not shake those residents, but if those same temperatures were to suddenly occur in Hawaii, Florida, Southern California, Mexico, Jamaica, or Saudi Arabia, it could be devastating for those regions. People, agriculture, utilities, and transportation aren't typically prepared for such a shift. And, when you add in the disastrous effects of extreme winter storms, the results can be crippling, even fatal!

More people die *during* heat waves than any other weather-related disaster, but more people die *from* cold waves than even heat waves when you take in the effects (and aftereffects) of the cold, including car accidents, the flu, pneumonia, etc. In other words, few people die after a heat wave ends, but after the cold snap leaves, cold-related deaths keep occurring. The effects of a cold wave tend to linger much longer than the actual wave itself.

Some people claim that heat waves target more of the sick, but cold waves and winter storms target more of the healthy. That might be true to some degree, but cold waves still cause higher than normal deaths among the elderly and the sick.

Much like heat waves, the extreme temperatures that cold waves produce can cause the elderly and the sick to experience problems such as heart attacks, strokes, and asthma attacks. This often happens because the cardiovascular and respiratory systems are strained while trying to keep the body temperature regulated.

Heat waves and cold waves are similar in other ways as well. Where heat waves cause the body to shut down with heat exhaustion, heat stroke, and then death, cold waves shut down the body with frostbite, hypothermia, and then death as well.

Hypothermia is dangerous, yet in a way, less dramatic than heat strokes (hyperthermia). Where you may vomit and convulse during heat strokes, with hypothermia, your body gets so cold that you stop shivering and your body ceases to produce its own heat. The blood minimizes its flow and grows colder in your extremities (like your arms, legs, and head) as your body attempts to preserve the temperature in the core of your body. This causes you to not think straight, act strangely, get tired, and even fall asleep in the cold, leading to death.

Hypothermia occurs because your body doesn't have enough resources to produce its own heat/energy. Even if you aren't hungry during a cold spell, keep eating, and wear enough clothing to keep warm, but not so much clothing that you perspire (sweat cools the body).

Cold waves can cause a variety of other problems as well. Crops can fail (creating a famine), livestock and wildlife can die from the cold and from starvation, and water mains can freeze or burst. The lack of water can cause health concerns and can limit the water needed for firefighting. Also, transportation gets crippled (cars won't start, ice on the roads, road congestion, etc.), rivers and lakes freeze over (barges and ships can't deliver products), and as people stay home from work and don't shop, local economies suffer.

BEFORE A COLD WAVE

1. Properly insulate internal and external plumbing to keep your water from freezing.
2. Know how to shut off water mains in case pipes freeze and then burst.
3. Stock up on food, water, and other necessities (including entertainment) in case you need to stay indoors for a while. Keep animals or livestock in mind as you do so.
4. Learn about frostbite and hypothermia and know how to treat each one.
5. Purchase adequate clothing, blankets, sleeping bags, and other supplies to be able to create warmth and stay warm, just in case utilities shut off.
6. Stock up on heaters, candles, matches, flashlights, fuel for cooking, and wood for fireplaces/stoves. Make sure open flames have ventilation to avoid carbon monoxide.
7. Winterize your home ahead of time (storm windows, extra insulations, etc.).
8. Winterize your vehicles (anti-freeze, etc.).
9. If you will be going away during very cold weather, leave the heater in your home set to 55°F (13°C) or higher to keep water in the pipes from freezing.

DURING A COLD WAVE

1. Protect yourself from frostbite and hypothermia by wearing warm, lightweight clothing in several layers. Stay indoors or out of the cold where possible.
2. If there are signs of frostbite (the skin and body tissue freezes – often the fingers, toes, earlobes, face, and the tip of the nose), then cover exposed skin or try to warm it, but not by rubbing the affected area, because you can damage the tissue. If it seems more severe, seek medical help immediately.
3. Look for signs of hypothermia. These include dangerously low body temperatures under 95°F (35°C), uncontrollable shivering followed by an absence of shivering, memory loss, disorientation, incoherence, slurred speech, drowsiness, and apparent exhaustion. If you recognize any of these symptoms, then remove all wet clothing and get the core of the body warmed by a fireplace, heater, warm water in a tub, or even body-to-body heat. Putting a person in blankets or sleeping bags alone won't work to rebuild their body heat. If the person is conscious, have them drink warm (non-alcoholic) drinks to warm the core of the body. Seek medical help quickly.
4. Keep water running through pipes (even slowly) if you think they may freeze.
5. Keep garage doors closed if there are water supply lines in the garage.

6. Open kitchen and bathroom cabinet doors to allow warmer air to circulate around the plumbing. Be sure to move any harmful cleaners and household chemicals out of the reach of children.

7. Keep your thermostat set to 55°F (13°C) or higher, both day and night, so pipes don't freeze overnight. A higher heating bill is cheaper than replacing burst pipes.

8. Shut off the water main if the pipes *do* burst.

9. If your house loses utilities and you can't stay warm, have a backup location to go to where you know will be warm (friend's house, church, public building, shelter, etc.).

10. Vulnerable crops may be sprayed with water. That will paradoxically protect the plants from freezing by absorbing the cold from surrounding air.

11. Due to the danger of carbon monoxide poisoning, never use a generator, grill, camp stove or other typical gasoline, propane, natural gas or charcoal-burning burning devices inside a home, garage, basement, crawlspace or any other enclosed area. Locate unit away from doors, windows and vents that could allow carbon monoxide to come indoors. Make sure all fireplaces and wood-burning stoves have a cleared chimney or pipe to the outside, allowing carbon monoxide and smoke an escape route.

12. Eat more meals, more often, and keep your body supplied with the energy it needs, even if you're in a hurry or don't feel hungry. In the cold, your body burns more calories and burns them faster.

13. Be aware of and help people who require special assistance such as elderly people living alone, people with disabilities, pregnant women, and children.

14. Bring pets inside or move other animals or livestock to sheltered areas with non-frozen drinking water available.

PREPARATION EXERCISE

After reading this section, what are some things you would like to do to better prepare yourself, your family, or your group for cold waves? (write in the section below)

How probable is this crisis a threat to you?
(✔one): □0 □1 □2 □3 □4 □5 □6 □7 □8 □9 □10
How long might this crisis last for you?
(✔one): □3days □3wks □3mos □6mos □1yr □+yrs
Possible nearby threats that concern you:
_____

_____

_____

_____

_____

_____

_____

Winter Storms

Winter storms can range from a moderate snow flurry over a few hours to a blinding blizzard lasting several days (covering houses and cars or even collapsing roofs). They may be small, affecting only a single community, or so large as to span over several states. Winter storms may be accompanied by dangerously low temperatures (cold waves) and also sometimes by strong winds, ice, hail, sleet, and freezing rain.

Most of us, sometime in our lives, will come across some form of a winter storm. So, how do you prepare?

BEFORE A WINTER STORM

1. Follow all the same recommendations found in the "Cold Wave" section of this book.
2. Purchase adequate ice melt, rock salt, or sand for your walkways.
3. Have snow shovels or other snow removal equipment on hand.

DURING A WINTER STORM

1. Follow all the same recommendations found in the "Cold Wave" section of this book.
2. Pay attention to the news for alerts and warnings.
3. Minimize travel, and if you do need to travel, make sure you have an emergency kit in your car (including food, water, and something to keep you warm). Travel in the daytime (when possible), stay on main roads, and try not to travel alone. Keep others informed of your schedule, destination, route, and when you expect to arrive. (If you don't arrive, then help can be sent along your predetermined route to find you.)
4. If you have a heart condition, don't overexert yourself while shoveling snow, etc.
5. Walk carefully on snowy or icy walkways, and wear footgear with a solid tread.
6. Keep dry and warm.
7. If you're caught in your car during a blizzard or slide off the highway or road, then do the following, where possible:
   o Pull off the highway so other moving cars can't pose a danger to yours.
   o Stay in the vehicle unless you see a close-by warm shelter or building you can easily get to. (Remember that snowstorms can distort distances, and the building may be further than you think.)
   o Turn on hazard lights and if in distress, hang a distress flag, shirt, or handkerchief from the antenna or window (the darker, the better).
   o Dress warmly and cover yourself with seat covers, maps, or anything you can

find to insulate yourself from the cold. Huddle with other passengers to share heat. Exercise slightly to keep your blood flowing and to stay warm but avoid sweating or overexertion.

o Even if you don't feel hungry, keep eating food and drinking fluids anyway (non-alcoholic beverages) to supply your body with energy. Remember, during the cold, your body burns more calories and burns them at a faster rate.

o Beware of alcoholic beverages. They make you *feel* warmer as they cause blood vessels to dilate, but they actually lower your body's core temperature.

o Run your engine and heater for about 10 minutes each hour to heat up the car (or longer if needed). While the car is running, make sure your exhaust pipes outside are clear and that you roll down the window very slightly for fresh air circulation. Avoid any carbon monoxide or carbon dioxide poisoning.

o If there is more than one of you, take turns sleeping. One person should be awake at all times to look for rescue crews.

o Limit use of electricity (car radio, lights, etc.) when the engine is off in order to conserve your battery.

o After the blizzard passes, drive away carefully (if you can), or wait for help, if stranded. If necessary and logical, leave the car and proceed on foot to safety. If stranded in a remote location, use nearby rocks, branches, or other materials in or outside your car to create a large "HELP" or "SOS" sign visible to rescue airplanes or other personnel. If you can't find any materials to use, then stamp a sign in the snow with your feet instead. Be creative!

PREPARATION EXERCISE

After reading this section, what are some things you would like to do to better prepare yourself, your family, or your group for winter storms? (write in the section below)

How probable is this crisis a threat to you?
(✔one): □0 □1 □2 □3 □4 □5 □6 □7 □8 □9 □10
How long might this crisis last for you?
(✔one): □3days □3wks □3mos □6mos □1yr □+yrs
Possible nearby threats that concern you:
_____

_____

_____

_____

_____

_____

_____

Thunderstorms

There are millions of thunderstorms (also known as Lightning or Electrical Storms) each year around the world. They are more common than most people think. Thunderstorms can produce hail, wind gusts, flash floods, wildfires, and much more, but they all have one thing in common: "lightning" (which actually causes the thunder sound).

Lightning is caused by static (usually from the movement of ice or rain within clouds), and as the static discharges, we see a flash of light or hear its thunderous sound. Lightning can reach temperatures near 54,000°F (30,000°C), can produce hundreds of millions of volts of electricity, and travel at speeds near one-third the speed of light.

There are 3 typical ways lightning occurs in thunderstorms: 1. Lightning that stays within one cloud (intra-cloud or IC), 2. Lightning that goes between clouds (cloud to cloud or CC), and 3. Lightning that travels between clouds and the ground (cloud and ground or CG). Lightning can also be created from the friction caused by volcanic eruptions, dust storms, snowstorms, forest fires, tornadoes, or anything else that causes static.

About 25% of lightning is Cloud and Ground (CG). When the lightning connects with the ground, it typically seeks out the shortest route to neutralize the static charge. This might be a tree, a tall building, or if very unlucky, a person.

Although most lightning victims actually survive the strike, lightning continues to be one of the top 3 storm-related killers worldwide. Those who do survive lightning, often report long-term, debilitating symptoms.

BEFORE A THUNDERSTORM

1. Discuss thunderstorm and lightning safety with all members of your household and pick a safe place in your home to gather away from windows, glass doors, skylights, metal, standing water, and concrete.
2. Get a battery or wind-up powered radio to listen to the news and prepare yourself for power outages.
3. Remove dead or rotting trees and branches that could fall and cause injury or damage during a severe thunderstorm.
4. If your house is right next to the tallest tree, pole, tower, or anything else in the neighborhood, you may consider taking extra precautions.

5. Remember, rubber-soled shoes and rubber tires provide NO protection from lightning.
6. Get trained in CPR.

DURING A THUNDERSTORM

1. Keep an eye on the sky. Look for darkening skies, flashes of lightning, increasing wind, and listen for thunder. Stay tuned to the local news.
2. If you see or hear a thunderstorm coming or your hair stands on end, get inside a completely enclosed building immediately! Remember the saying: "If You Can Hear It, Clear It and If You Can See It, Flee It." Stay away from windows and off porches. Don't lean on concrete walls or lie down on concrete floors because of the metal rebar inside.
3. If indoors, avoid plumbing and water (both can conduct electricity). Don't wash dishes, run the dishwasher or laundry, or take a shower or bath until the storm passes. Also, avoid using plugged in electronic devices like hair dryers, etc.
4. Postpone outdoor activities. Many people struck by lightning aren't even in the area where rain is falling.
5. If no enclosed building is convenient, stay or get inside a hard-topped all-metal vehicle, and make sure you don't touch anything metal while inside. (The enclosed metal of a car acts as a type of Faraday cage and dissipates the electricity on the outside and keeps you safe on the inside.)
6. If outside, avoid metal! Don't lean against metal vehicles, towers, poles, etc. Get off bicycles, motorcycles, tractors, farm equipment, golf carts, or metal bleachers. Don't hold on to metal items such as golf clubs, tools, or pipes. Large metal objects can attract lightning, and small metal objects can cause burns.
7. If outside, be the lowest point. Lightning hits the tallest object. Stay far away from trees, electric towers, etc. Try to get over twice as far away as the tallest object is tall. Stay off hills and away from open fields (where you become the tallest object!).
8. If outside, keep your feet close together (so electricity can't flow up one leg and down the other), and stay away from other people (don't huddle).
9. Get away from and out of water (it's a great conductor of electricity). Stay off the beach or out of small boats, canoes, kayaks, etc. Lightning can travel long distances in water (deep and wide). Don't drive through flooded areas or play in puddles.
10. To determine the distance of lightning in miles, count the seconds between the flash and the thunder and divide by 5. Five seconds = about 1 mile (1.6 kilometers) away. The danger zone is anything within 10 miles (roughly 50 seconds of counting).
11. To preserve your electronics (computers, televisions, etc.), have them plugged into a surge suppressor ahead of time, or unplug them completely until the storm passes. Turn off your air-conditioners, if possible, so they don't attract the electric charge.
12. Stay away from downed power lines and report them immediately.
13. Protect yourself & your valuables from large hail and keep your animals safe as well.
14. If someone gets struck by lightning, call 9-1-1 to get immediate help, and if possible, check the following:
    o **Breathing** - if breathing has stopped, begin mouth-to-mouth resuscitation.
    o **Heartbeat** - if the heart has stopped, administer CPR.
    o **Injuries** - be aware of other possible injuries, such as nervous-system damage, broken bones, and loss of hearing or eyesight. Check for burns where the lightning entered and left the body. You may choose to provide assistance within your capabilities.

PREPARATION EXERCISE

After reading this section, what are some things you would like to do to better prepare yourself, your family, or your group for thunderstorms? (write in the section below)

How probable is this crisis a threat to you?
(✔one): □0 □1 □2 □3 □4 □5 □6 □7 □8 □9 □10
How long might this crisis last for you?
(✔one): □3days □3wks □3mos □6mos □1yr □+yrs
Possible nearby threats that concern you:
_____

_____

_____

_____

_____

_____

_____

_____

_____

_____

_____

_____

_____

_____

_____

_____

_____

_____

Tsunamis

The name "tsunami" is Japanese and means "harbor (or port) wave." In the open sea, a tsunami goes generally unnoticed, but the destructive force is quite apparent once its rising waters hit the shallowness of harbors.

Tsunamis happen when earthquakes, underwater landslides (yes, there are mountains underwater), volcanic eruptions, meteorites, or similar events, suddenly displace large amounts of water. By the way, since the wave was caused by something other than raising or lowering tides, it's not considered a "tidal wave."

The sheer force of tsunamis is baffling. Tsunamis can travel across entire oceans with limited energy loss, especially in deep waters, and can reach speeds of about 500 miles (or 805 kilometers) per hour, almost as fast as a jet plane. As a tsunami approaches land, the shallow water slows the wave down but also causes coastal areas to flood quickly as the water rises.

The first wave to hit is usually not the strongest as successive waves get bigger and stronger. Waves can continue to hit for 24 hours and each wave alone may last from 5-60 minutes, depending on the wavelength.

Since awareness is half the battle to being prepared, let's become more aware of tsunamis, how to recognize them, and what to do if caught in one at home or on vacation.

INTERESTING TSUNAMI FACTS

The Tallest Recorded Tsunami happened the night of July 9, 1958 in Lituya Bay, Alaska. An earthquake loosened a 3000-foot mass of rock that came crashing into the ocean, causing a large wave. As the tsunami began to hit land about a mile away, the water rose 1,720 feet high (almost 300 feet higher than the tip of the Empire State Building) and then continued for miles down the coast reaching heights in the hundreds of feet.

It's hard to imagine, but with all the earthquakes in Alaska, it's not unreasonable to believe there are many more Alaskan tsunamis to come, maybe not as tall, but still large enough to do a lot of damage along coastlines, even hundreds of miles away.

The Worst Tsunami Disaster happened on December 26th, 2004 when a 9.1-magnitude earthquake shook for 8-10 minutes near Sumatra, Indonesia. The fault zone, about 810 miles long, caused waves over 160 feet in height, and when they hit land, they reached about 3 miles inland in some areas. Even though the waves took hours to reach many of the coastlines, there were no warning systems in place, and in the end, sadly 230,000 people in 14 countries were reported dead.

What makes it even more devastating is watching the videos of tourist families on the beaches seeing the water recede and even following it, enjoying the day, amazed at the exposed sea floor. Because they lacked the understanding, they were completely unaware of the coming danger.

Tsunami Warning Signs

1. An earthquake offshore or felt under your feet is a natural first warning that a tsunami may hit within minutes. If you're within 3 miles of large bodies of water (even large lakes), get to higher ground and tune into the news until you're sure there's no risk.
2. Tsunamis originating inland can travel up rivers and streams. After an earthquake, stay away from the shores of large rivers as you would stay away from the beach and ocean.
3. Sometimes tsunamis are preceded by a noticeable fall or rise of the water level. If something seems strange in the water's patterns or if the water recedes more than normal or unusually quickly (called "drawback"), don't take your chances. A receding ocean is about a 5-minute warning to evacuate.
4. A tsunami may also occur with very little oceanic warning or drawback.
5. Keep your ears peeled and listen! Many witnesses have said that a tsunami sounds thunderous, like a freight train coming or like a sucking sound.
6. Animals (including fish) sometimes behave strangely or move toward or away from the ocean in groups.
7. Remember that the first waves to hit aren't the most powerful. Sometimes people mistake the first wave as normal but then get captured by the following, stronger waves, and can't escape.

Tsunami Danger Zones

The most dangerous areas for tsunamis worldwide are mainly countries that have the Pacific or Indian Oceans touching their shores. Many of these areas fall within the famous "Ring of Fire" that is well-known for its constant tectonic movement and volcanic activity.

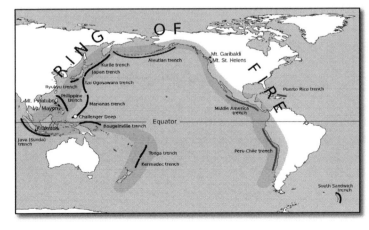

Other big caution zones worldwide include the Mediterranean Sea and the European and Northern African Atlantic Ocean coastlines. Countries like Greece are historically known for being earthquake zones and tectonic movements off the coast of Portugal have caused massive tsunamis in the past that have traveled as far as North and South America.

In the U.S., the states of Hawaii, Alaska, Washington, Oregon, and California have the highest risks. An earthquake right off their coasts could cause a tsunami so close that residents would have little time to evacuate and so powerful that millions could be in danger.

The U.S. East Coast and the Gulf of Mexico face local threats as well, though usually not as serious or apparent. Fracture zones in the Caribbean and the Atlantic as well as underwater landslides threaten these areas.

For example, in 1929, a 7.2-magnitude earthquake off the coast of Newfoundland (just north of the United States) created a tsunami that killed 28 people. In 1918, a Puerto Rican 7.5-magnitude earthquake formed a tsunami nearly 20-feet high that caused 116 deaths. In 2010, a Haitian earthquake created a local tsunami that hit Haiti's banks within minutes.

In short, whether it's due to earthquakes, volcanoes, underwater landslides, or even a meteorite hitting the earth, if you live within 3 miles of an ocean coast or if you live near very large bodies of water besides oceans (especially in earthquake territories), take the precautions you need against possible tsunamis.

BEFORE A TSUNAMI

1. Find out if your home, workplace, school, or other places you normally visit are in a tsunami hazard zone. If so, find out each city's evacuation plan (or create one).
2. If you're in or visit tsunami hazard zones, know the distance between each location and the ocean, lake, or river shore. Also, know how high above or below sea level (or other water body levels) you are. This will help you assess the danger better.
3. Create and practice your own evacuation plans. Try to get 3 or more miles (5+ kilometers) away from the coastline and 100 or more feet (30 meters) above water levels, if possible.
4. If time is short, practice getting to the 3rd floor of a sturdy building or to a roof instead.
5. If you're a vacationer, when visiting a place that could experience tsunamis, use these same precaution and preparation steps.

DURING A TSUNAMI

1. If you hear Tsunami sirens or warnings, don't procrastinate. Act quickly!
2. Get as far inland as possible and get to stable, higher ground as soon as possible.
3. Help warn others to do the same.
4. Avoid being near power lines.
5. Try not to get wet in order to avoid hypothermia.
6. If you get caught in a tsunami, unless you obviously know you can get to safety, save your strength and don't fight against it. Try to find something that floats, get on, and hold onto it until either someone rescues you or you can finally get to safety.

AFTER A TSUNAMI

1. Keep your radios tuned to the news for further warnings.
2. Check yourself and others for injuries and get help, if needed.
3. Avoid buildings that have water around them because they may be structurally weakened.
4. Stay away from downed power lines, broken gas lines, and sewage.
5. Drink only clean water to avoid diseases and sickness.

PREPARATION EXERCISE

After reading this section, what are some things you would like to do to better prepare yourself, your family, or your group for tsunamis? (write in the section below)

How probable is this crisis a threat to you?
(✔one): □0 □1 □2 □3 □4 □5 □6 □7 □8 □9 □10
How long might this crisis last for you?
(✔one): □3days □3wks □3mos □6mos □1yr □+yrs
Possible nearby threats that concern you:
_____

_____

_____

_____

_____

_____

_____

_____

_____

_____

_____

_____

Volcanoes

I remember when Mt. St. Helens in Washington erupted back in 1980. Ash reached 11 of the 50 United States. As a boy, I stood amazed at ash falling all around in Southern California (about 900 miles south of the actual volcano, two states away!). I think that was the first time I began to realize the sheer power of volcanoes and how far reaching their grasps are.

For example, in 1815, Indonesia (halfway around the world) experienced the largest volcanic eruption to occur in over 1300 years. Its far-reaching effects were experienced all over the world, and the following year was called the infamous "Year Without a Summer." Crops failed, food shortages abounded, and over 1800 people, including many Americans, froze to death because of climate changes globally. Volcanoes can affect you, even if you live thousands of miles away from one.

In honor of photojournalist Reid Turner Blackburn who lost his life in the Mt. St. Helen's eruption. This is his car.

There is volcanic activity (or at least hotspots) in most every country around the world. Just in the United States alone, there are nearly 170 geologically active volcanoes. Fifty-five of those have a threat level of "high" and 18 have a status of "very high." As an example, I've listed the "very high" ones below, along with the dates of their last eruptions:

Akutan Volcano, AK - Erupted 1992
Augustine Volcano, AK – In Unrest Now
Makushin Volcano, AK - Erupted 1995
Redoubt Volcano, AK - Erupted 1990
Spurr Volcano, AK- Erupted 1992
Lassen Peak, CA - Erupted 1917
Long Valley, CA – Erupted Pleistocene Era
Mount Shasta, CA – Erupted 1786
Kilauea Volcano, HA- In Unrest Now

Mauna Loa Volcano, HA – Erupted 1984
Crater Lake, OR – Erupted ±2290 BC
Mount Hood, OR - Erupted 1866
Newberry Volcano, OR Erupted 620 AD
South Sister, OR - Erupted 50 BC (?)
Mount Baker Volcano, WA - Erupted 1880
Glacier Peak, WA – Erupted ±1700.
Mount Rainier, WA– Erupted 1825.
Mount St. Helens, WA – In Unrest Now

If you live near a known volcano, active or dormant, you need to understand what happens during a volcano. Volcanoes can blast hot solid and molten rock fragments, deadly hot ash, and suffocating gases into the air that can travel hundreds of miles. The ground shakes, wildfires abound, and several flash floods, mudflows, and landslides often take place.

Rapid flooding and mudflows typically happen because hot ash or lava from the eruption can rapidly melt snow and ice surrounding the volcano. The water quickly mixes with falling ash, soil, and other debris in its pathway, and can travel 20 to 40 miles per hour as a river of mud that can stretch up to 50 miles away from the actual volcano itself.

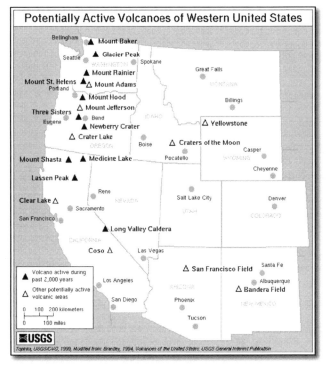

So, what do you do to prepare for volcanoes?

BEFORE A VOLCANO

1. Know where the closest volcanic activity is to your location and understand how it might affect you.
2. Make evacuation plans. If you live in a known volcanic hazard area, plan an escape route as well as a backup route.
3. If you live within 200 miles of a volcano, buy respiratory masks to protect yourself from breathing in ash, other particles, or harmful gases.
4. Create 72-hour emergency kits and emergency plans for quick evacuation.
5. If you think you might be forced to stay indoors (to avoid breathing in ash and gases), build up your food and water storage, and prepare your other needs in order to live without access to public utilities, food, and water for a period of time.
6. Be prepared for several large earthquakes, mudflows, landslides, moving rocks, flash floods, thick ash, poisonous air, acid rain, and even tsunamis.

DURING A VOLCANO

1. Listen to the news and pay attention (use your portable radio if needed).
2. Stay out of the area defined as a restricted zone by government officials. Trying to watch an erupting volcano up close is a bad idea because of deadly gas, hot ash, flying debris, and more. Evacuate as soon as advised to do so and get as far away as possible.
3. If you're unable to evacuate, protect yourself from falling ash by remaining indoors. Close all outside doors, windows, and vents (chimney, furnaces, air conditioners, fans, and other vents) until the ash settles. Stay indoors (if possible) and wait for help, unless there's a danger of the roof collapsing, etc.
4. If needed, do your best to clear away heavy ash from flat or low-pitched roofs that may cave in, but remember to wear a mask, goggles, and other protection as you do so.
5. If you see water levels begin to rise in a stream or river, quickly move to higher ground and stay off bridges. Avoid river valleys and low-lying areas as a rule of thumb.

6. If you see or hear the crashing sounds of a mudflow, even if you can't see it, move perpendicular to the flow direction and get to higher ground as quickly as possible.
7. Mudflows can move faster than you can walk or run. Look upstream before crossing a bridge and don't cross the bridge if a mudflow is approaching.
8. Keep in mind that large rainfalls may later mix with ash deposits and result in additional mudflows.
9. Remember to help infants, elderly people, and people with special needs around you.
10. If you need to go outside or travel away from the blast, wear long-sleeved shirts, long pants, sturdy boots, goggles, respiratory masks, and hats to protect yourself from the gases and ashes.
11. If you don't have a dust mask, hold or tie a damp cloth or bandana over your mouth and nose to help with breathing.
12. Stay away from areas downwind from the volcano to avoid volcanic ashes and gases.
13. Avoid driving in heavy ash-fall unless absolutely necessary. If you have to drive, keep speed down to 35 MPH or slower since ashes gets stirred up and can cause the engine to clog and stall.
14. Bring animals and livestock into closed shelters.

PREPARATION EXERCISE

After reading this section, what are some things you would like to do to better prepare yourself, your family, or your group for volcanic eruptions? (write in the section below)

How probable is this crisis a threat to you?
(✔one): □0 □1 □2 □3 □4 □5 □6 □7 □8 □9 □10
How long might this crisis last for you?
(✔one): □3days □3wks □3mos □6mos □1yr □+yrs
Possible nearby threats that concern you:
_____

_____

_____

_____

_____

_____

_____

_____

_____

Debris Flows
(Avalanches, Landslides, Rockslides, Mudslides, Sinkholes)

If you live on or near a hill, a mountain, a cliff, or a location prone to sinkholes, then debris flows should be on your list of concerns.

Debris flows (land, mud, rock, or snow) happen for a number of reasons. These include earthquakes, volcanoes, heavy rain or snowfall, rapid snowmelt, post-fire erosion, broken water pipes, and the wearing down of sediments caused by underground lakes, rivers, or waterways. Debris flows even can happen simply from the expanding and contracting of the ground (from hot and cold temperatures) or just from gravity over time.

Debris flows can strike with or without warning. They can travel as slow as a turtle or as rapid as a sports car. They can shift only a few feet or travel for miles from their source while picking up houses, buildings, cars, trees, large boulders, and more along the path.

BEFORE A DEBRIS FLOW

1. Observe and become familiar with the land around you. Are trees progressively leaning more and more over time? Is there any strange bulging at the bottom of a hill? Are there any potential dangers that you haven't noticed before? Have any occurrences happened in the past in your area? If so, make sure you know what they are because if it's happened before, there's a good chance it'll happen again.
2. Get a ground assessment of your property.
3. Watch and be aware of changes in and around your home. Are doors or windows sticking or jamming for the first time? Are there new cracks forming in bricks, walls, tile, plasters, or in the foundation? Have any underground pipes or utility lines broken without reason? Are any of the outside pavements collapsing or sloping suddenly?
4. Avoid building near steep slopes, cliffs, and ledges. Be aware of any natural or man-made rivers or drainage systems nearby that may seep into the ground near your property and create instability.
5. Protect hills and slopes by planting vegetation including trees, shrubs, and grasses.
6. Build retaining walls, if necessary.
7. Check online or at the city/county for geological data and historical damage caused by underground water or limestone deposits. You can also use Google and Google Images to search the term "sinkholes in the United States" to see if you're in a danger zone.
8. If you're in a location that may experience avalanches, check the local warnings, buy and wear an avalanche beacon, and if you are traveling or away from home near a

danger zone, advise a friend or family member where you will be exactly and when you will return. Report back when you arrive or if your circumstances change immediately.

9. Make sure you put your avalanche beacon in a very secure place (like a zippered pocket) that won't get jarred loose if you're hit by an avalanche.

DURING DEBRIS FLOW THREATS

1. Especially during a storm, heavy rain, heavy snowfall, or after an earthquake, if there's any doubt in your mind of danger, listen to your gut, and get out.
2. If you hear a faint rumbling sound that's noticeably increasing in volume, or if you hear trees cracking, boulders clicking together, or any similar sound, don't take your chances, and leave the area immediately.
3. Keep alert at night and be aware that many people die in their sleep from debris flows.
4. Where possible, during and right after a storm, stay away from low-lying areas (like valleys). Stay off bridges and away from flowing water (especially near steep inclines or in valleys). A mudslide or mudflow can move faster than you can run and can catch you by surprise.
5. If you're near a stream or other form of moving water, pay attention to the water. If the water suddenly increases in height and flow or if the water changes from clear to muddy, quickly get to higher ground.
6. If you get caught in a mudslide, and it seems possible, run up the slide and off to the side as fast as you can. If escape isn't possible, curl up in a tight ball with your arms covering your head to protect it from debris.

If You're Caught in an Avalanche

1. Keep your avalanche beacon securely on you at all times.
2. If the avalanche starts right under your feet, try running uphill and/or to the side to get off the fracturing slab of snow.
3. If you're on a snowmobile, continue in the direction you were going and increase your speed to get off the sliding snow as quickly as possible. If it is too late to escape, then abandon the snowmobile. You want to be as light and buoyant as possible in order to increase your chances of staying on top of the snow.
4. If you're on skis or a snowboard, head downhill first to gather some speed then veer to the side as soon as you can to get off the moving snow.

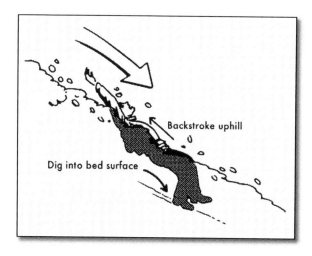

5. If the avalanche takes you, stay on top of the avalanche as much as you can by "swimming" a backstroke uphill. If swimming is too tough, then you can violently

thrash around in order to avoid sinking. Do whatever it takes to stay on top of the sliding snow.

6. As you move around, try to keep at least one arm reaching for the sky. This may be easier said than done, but it increases the chances for rescuers to find you once the snow settles and may help you know which direction is up, so you can dig yourself out better.

7. Create an air pocket. As soon as the slide starts to come to a standstill, move back and forth and put an arm (or two, if needed) in front of your face to create as much breathing space as possible in front of your face. Take in a deep breath and expand your chest as much as you can, also to create space.

8. Spit! When you are being tumbled around in the snow and covered, you often lose orientation, and what you think is up, actually isn't. Once the slide has come to a halt, spit and pay attention to the direction the spit goes. Using gravity as your friend, spit will tell you which direction is down. Then, if possible, try to dig yourself out of the snow in the opposite direction (up!). Learn to spit, and don't waste any precious time or energy digging the wrong way.

9. Stay Calm. By getting nervous and breathing faster, you use up what little oxygen you may have around you. It's natural to panic, but you must keep your wits about you in this situation. Typically, before the snow begins to pack any further, you have about a 15-minute window to keep creating air pockets around your face and keep digging yourself out if possible.

10. If you can't move very much, and you know which way is up, do what you can to push an arm or leg in that direction. Hopefully you will break the surface and help rescuers find you faster.

PREPARATION EXERCISE

After reading this section, what are some things you would like to do to better prepare yourself, your family, or your group for debris flows? (write in the section below)

How probable is this crisis a threat to you?
(✔one): ☐0 ☐1 ☐2 ☐3 ☐4 ☐5 ☐6 ☐7 ☐8 ☐9 ☐10

How long might this crisis last for you?
(✔one): ☐3days ☐3wks ☐3mos ☐6mos ☐1yr ☐+yrs

Possible nearby threats that concern you:

_____

_____

_____

_____

_____

Outbreaks & Pandemics

The Bubonic Plague of 1346 AD killed up to 70% of Europe. The 1545 Mexico fever left 80% of that country's citizens (millions of people) dead. In the 1850s, over 1 million Russians were killed by cholera. About 50 million people worldwide died because of the 1918 flu. Because our world today is much more interconnected than in the past, disease is able to travel faster than ever before, going from an outbreak to a worldwide pandemic in no time. Here are a few preparedness tips to consider:

1. Follow all 7 of the Prep Steps in order to have enough food, water, medicines, and other supplies on hand to remain indoors until danger passes.
2. Avoid close contact with people, especially those who are sick. Likewise, if you become sick, keep your distance from others, and stay home, if possible.
3. Cover your mouth and nose with a tissue or arm sleeve when coughing or sneezing.
4. Wash your hands often to help protect yourself from germs. Avoid touching your eyes, nose, or mouth (germs often spread when a person touches something that's contaminated with germs and then touches his or her eyes, nose, or mouth).
5. Stay healthy – get enough sleep, exercise, stress less, eat well, and drink lots of water.

PREPARATION EXERCISE

After reading this section, what are some things you would like to do to better prepare yourself, your family, or your group for epidemics? (write in the section below)

How probable is this crisis a threat to you?
(✔one): □0 □1 □2 □3 □4 □5 □6 □7 □8 □9 □10
How long might this crisis last for you?
(✔one): □3days □3wks □3mos □6mos □1yr □+yrs
Possible nearby threats that concern you:
_____

_____

_____

_____

_____

_____

Solar Storms & Meteorites

Threats from outer space are just as real as the crises we face daily here on Earth. Two of these threats from space are coronal mass ejections (CMEs) from the sun and meteorites.

A CME is an intense burst of plasma and magnetic energy coming from solar storms, which if aimed at Earth, threaten satellites in orbit and the power grids of every nation. Solar storms are our solar system's largest explosive events and can last from a few minutes to many hours.

For example, the Carrington Event of 1859 was a coronal mass ejection whose rays hit Earth and blew out telegraph systems all over Europe and North America, giving some telegraph operators electric shocks and even causing fires. A similar CME happened in 2012, but luckily, its rays missed the Earth by about 7 days. Today, with our dependence on power grids, if it *had* hit the Earth, millions (if not billions) could have eventually lost their lives.

Like Hollywood loves to remind us, asteroids, comets, and meteorites also pose threats to Earth in a variety of ways. A meteorite just a few miles big, hitting the earth, can produce the destructive energy equivalent to several millions of nuclear weapons detonating at the same time. That could change weather patterns, poison the air, cause tsunamis, and much more.

So, how do you prepare for something so unpredictable? Here's my suggestion:
1. Unplug and turn off all electronic equipment until the threat passes.
2. Follow the 7 Prep Steps to make sure you have food, water, and other supplies in place.

PREPARATION EXERCISE

After reading this section, what are some things you would like to do to better prepare yourself, your family, or your group against these threats? (write in the section below)

How probable is this crisis a threat to you?
(✔one): □0 □1 □2 □3 □4 □5 □6 □7 □8 □9 □10
How long might this crisis last for you?
(✔one): □3days □3wks □3mos □6mos □1yr □+yrs
Possible nearby threats that concern you:
_____

_____

_____

_____

_____

MAN-MADE CRISES

Man-made disasters vary in nature and type. Below is a short list of the more common concerns. Review them and consider the ones that seem more probable in your lifetime.

As you continue through the rest of the 7 Prep Steps in this book, you'll learn how to better prepare for man-made disasters. In the meanwhile, let's learn a little bit about each of the following different possible crises.

Financial – Financial threats are probably the most common man-made crises we face. We're all familiar with people out of work and struggling financially in one way or another, yet there are financial threats that are much greater and further reaching than just personal job loss.

How probable is this crisis a threat to you?
(✔one): □0 □1 □2 □3 □4 □5 □6 □7 □8 □9 □10
How long might this crisis last for you?
(✔one): □3days □3wks □3mos □6mos □1yr □+yrs
Possible nearby threats that concern you:
_____

In today's world, we face national and global economic threats more than ever before. We live in a time when the world markets are completely intertwined. What happens in Greece affects Europe, what happens in Europe affects the United States, and what happens in the United States affects the world. Nations going deeper in debt, pandemics slowing down economies, mass job loses, a derivative market bubble near one quadrillion-dollars (more money than all the world's economies combined), put us at risk, making this threat very real.

With the United States losing its AAA credit rating in 2011 and with skyrocketing national debts, the world is losing its confidence in the U.S. dollar. Things get even worse when you consider how aging baby-boomers will depend on un-funded U.S. liabilities (such as Medicare, Medicaid, and Social Security) that are currently at over a hundred trillion dollars.

Worldwide, nations have become highly dependent on credit and debt. A large hike in interest rates or sudden credit restrictions these days could cripple not only nations, but states, cities, families, and individuals for decades to come. What steps can you take to protect yourself and your family from an unpredictable economic future?

Hazardous Materials – Do you live near any manufacturers that use chemicals that may enter water supplies? Are there any Nuclear power plants nearby? Are there nearby businesses that if they caught fire could fill the air with toxic substances?

How probable is this crisis a threat to you?
(✔one): □0 □1 □2 □3 □4 □5 □6 □7 □8 □9 □10
How long might this crisis last for you?
(✔one): □3days □3wks □3mos □6mos □1yr □+yrs
Possible nearby threats that concern you:
_____

Terrorism – The scariest part about terrorists is that you don't know how, when, or where they'll attack. Terrorists will use bombings, biological threats, water supply contaminations, psychological warfare, and so much more, suddenly, without notice. For example, two of the biggest terrorist threats that face any country are EMP attacks and cyber-attacks.

EMP ATTACKS: Probably the biggest threat facing developed countries is an Electromagnetic Magnetic Pulse (EMP) attack (or other mass attack on a nation's electric grid).

An EMP attack occurs when a nuclear device is detonated high in the atmosphere and sends an electronic pulse strong enough to fry electronics of all types.

Just a missile or two detonated high enough above the United States can send the entire nation back 200 years in technology. Most computers, cell phones, communication, manufacturing, banking, cars, trucks, airplanes, running water, gas, and electricity could cease to function in seconds.

> **How probable is this crisis a threat to you?**
> (✔one): □0 □1 □2 □3 □4 □5 □6 □7 □8 □9 □10
> **How long might this crisis last for you?**
> (✔one): □3days □3wks □3mos □6mos □1yr □+yrs
> **Possible nearby threats that concern you:**
> _____

The United States EMP Commission, in 2008, estimated that within 12 months of a nationwide blackout, up to 90% of the U.S. population could possibly perish from starvation, disease, and societal breakdown. We take for granted how much we depend on electricity.

CYBER ATTACKS: A major cyber-attack on the Internet could send our economy spiraling downward. We've grown so dependent on the Internet for travel, banking, communication, business, record keeping, and so much more. How would our economy survive in the short or in the long run if the Internet were sabotaged?

Cyber-attacks also include hacking a nation's utilities and turning them off remotely with a damaging computer virus. If gas, electricity, and/or water were shut down, even for a month or two, the consequences can be devastating. Millions could suffer and die.

 **Civil Unrest** – Riots, panic, etc. If you live in a large city or a place that experiences higher than normal crime rates, it doesn't take much for civil unrest to begin. During a major crisis, whether natural or man-made, people and

> **How probable is this crisis a threat to you?**
> (✔one): □0 □1 □2 □3 □4 □5 □6 □7 □8 □9 □10
> **How long might this crisis last for you?**
> (✔one): □3days □3wks □3mos □6mos □1yr □+yrs
> **Possible nearby threats that concern you:**
> _____

groups can get violent, especially if people can't feed their families or enough people lose their jobs. Just something as controversial as racial differences, politics, or economics can cause riots to spread and perpetuate. As one emergency preparation expert put it, "you're always 72 hours away from a riot." Desperate or angry people can become dangerous quickly.

 **War** - Though it's hard to imagine in many countries, there may come a day when foreign troops attack and occupy parts of your country. War comes in all forms, including chemical, nuclear, etc. During wartime, you may lose access to a lot of the freedoms and privileges you now enjoy.

How probable is this crisis a threat to you?
(✔one): □0 □1 □2 □3 □4 □5 □6 □7 □8 □9 □10
How long might this crisis last for you?
(✔one): □3days □3wks □3mos □6mos □1yr □+yrs
Possible nearby threats that concern you:
_____

 **Zombie Attacks** – What's a good preparedness book without mentioning zombies, eh?! Haha.

How probable is this crisis a threat to you?
(✔one): □0 □1 □2 □3 □4 □5 □6 □7 □8 □9 □10
How long might this crisis last for you?
(✔one): □3days □3wks □3mos □6mos □1yr □+yrs
Possible nearby threats that concern you:
_____

PREPARATION EXERCISE

After reading this section, are there any other man-made threats that come to mind for you personally? List them here.

_____

_____

What are some things you would like to do to better prepare yourself, your family, or your group for man-made disasters? (write in the section below)

_____

_____

_____

_____

_____

PrepStep #2

72-HOUR PREPAREDNESS

A sage traveling all day is *never* far from the supplies in his cart, and
however spectacular the views, he remains calm and composed.
- *Lao Tzu, Tao Te China*

72-HOUR PREPAREDNESS

Good job so far getting through the Risk Assessment section by identifying and then taking the time to really understand your biggest risks!

The work you did in PrepStep #1 will help you continue the rest of the 7 Prep Steps the right way and not waste time and money doing it wrong. Feel free to go back and reference PrepStep #1 as often as needed as you continue through the rest of this course.

(If you skipped over the PrepStep #1, do yourself and your family a favor, and go back and get it done before proceeding to PrepStep #2.)

Sometimes the first few minutes, hours, or days of an emergency situation—in the stress of a sudden crisis—the biggest mistakes are made, and lives are lost. The goal of PrepStep #2 is to make sure you know how to act (not react) in these situations and to make sure your loved ones survive the first 3 days of any sudden emergency.

72-hour preparedness is MUCH more than simply having a survival kit (bug-out bag). These kits are a part of your preparation, but they are only a small part of your 3-day emergency preparations.

In order to really survive, you will also need to create emergency plans from the notes you took in PrepStep #1 and then identify the knowledge and skills you need to make those plans work.

Knowing what to do before the crisis is what really saves lives.

On March 27th, 1977, Pan Am Flight 1736 was hit by a KLM plane taking off on the foggy Los Rodeos Airport runway on the Spanish island of Tenerife.

Because passenger Paul Heck immediately knew what to do to survive, he grabbed his wife Floy and dragged her down the smoky aisle out through a hole on the left side of plane and jumped to safety.

Floy said she was like a zombie being pulled by her husband, and as she passed through the plane, she saw her close friend Lorraine still sitting in her seat looking forward stunned, with her jaw slightly opened and her hands in her lap, not knowing what to do.

There were only about 60 seconds before the plane went up in flames, and because Paul knew where the exits were and knew what to do in an emergency fire, he and Floy made it out alive while 344 people, including Loraine, died.

It was a very sad event, yet this event shows how just a little preparation can help you live through any sudden emergency (e.g., fires, earthquakes, tornadoes, floods, terrorist threats, chemical spills, riots, avalanches, etc.)

Surviving the first 3 seconds to 3 days of a sudden crisis is what PrepStep #2 is all about.

In this section, we're going to focus on 3 things:

1. First, using what you learned in the risk assessment section, you're going to create (or purchase) emergency "grab-and-go" kits and other emergency supplies specific to the risks you identified in PrepStep #1. These include home, car, work, and/or school kits.

2. Next, you're going to create emergency plans that deal with those specific emergencies.

3. Finally, I'm going to encourage you to practice those plans and build your emergency preparedness skills (which is more than 99% of people ever do).

If you're willing, you can also make practice a tradition each year until knowing exactly what to do in any disaster becomes second nature to you and your family - everyone comes out alive.

With this in mind, let's set some goals to help you complete your **72-Hour Preparedness** (PrepStep #2).

Write in a goal date for each action item in the list below, and pick completion dates that are realistic enough to fit your time availability and budget.

Commit to accomplish each section as soon as possible.

SET YOUR "EMERGENCY 72-HOUR PREPARATION" GOAL DATES:

✓ Create (or Buy) Your 72-Hour Emergency Kits. (Goal Date: _____)

✓ Create Your Emergency Plans. (Goal Date: _____)

✓ Practice Your Emergency Plans for the First Time. (Goal Date: _____)

Goal 1: Create Your 72-Hour Kits (or Buy the Right Ones)

Most people buy an emergency kit BEFORE even figuring out what types of items they really need in their kits. In fact, most people purchase a pre-made kit without really knowing what to do with everything in their kits (and sometimes don't know what they even purchased).

Don't get me wrong, having some sort of kit is better than having no kit at all, but wouldn't it be better to customize kits that ACTUALLY WORK to fit your needs?

Because everyone's situation is different, and each person has different emergency needs, a "one-size-fits-all" kit isn't always the best solution.

If you're willing to customize kits to your needs, let's start with listing the types of natural and man-made emergency situations you think you would need a kit for.

List the crisis situations from PrepStep #1 that require emergency kits:

☐ _____   ☐ _____

☐ _____   ☐ _____

☐ _____   ☐ _____

☐ _____   ☐ _____

☐ _____   ☐ _____

(Later on, after you've finished creating your kits, come back to your list above and if the kits are sufficient to fit your needs, use the check boxes to mark each off as "completed.")

Number of Kits Needed

Ideally, you should create a 72-hour kit for each person in your family or group (though you may need to double up kits to help out infants, small children, or people with special needs).

In the sections below, what are all the separate kits you want to create? List all the people, vehicles, or situations that you need kits for:

Home Kits Needed:	Work/School Kits:	Car Kits Needed:
_____	_____	_____
_____	_____	_____
_____	_____	_____
_____	_____	_____
_____	_____	_____
_____	_____	_____
_____	_____	_____
_____	_____	_____
_____	_____	_____

BUILDING OR PICKING THE RIGHT KITS

As you consider the lists you filled out on the previous page, use the information in the following pages to decide what products you want in each of your kits. The exercises in this section will also help you decide whether you should create your own kits or purchase them pre-built from a supplier.

By the end of PrepStep #2, you'll know exactly which supplies you'll need in your kits in order to meet your individual, family, or group needs.

Make your kits simple or make them as elaborate and individualized as you choose (e.g., different for children than adults, different for home than for work, etc.).

Let's get started with the first priority, 72-hour water preparation...

72 HOURS OF WATER

In an emergency situation, some precautions and preparations are obviously more important than others. For example, preparedness experts use the Rule of 3's to prepare for survival situations. The Rule of 3's says that in an emergency situation, you can die in:

> **3 seconds** without hope
> **3 minutes** without air
> **3 hours** without heat
> **3 days** without water
> **3 weeks** without food

In any crisis, water is more important than food in priority. You can survive for 3 weeks drinking *only* water, but your vital organs can fail within 3 days without it.

Yet, even more important than water, is clean water. In many disasters, there's plenty of water around, just not clean water. Even city water may look clean coming out of your faucet but be dangerously contaminated without you knowing.

If you're thirsty enough, you'll drink anything! Water contaminated with traces of sewage, fuels, chemicals, or harmful bacteria can cause vomiting, diarrhea, dehydration, fevers, and sicknesses of all sorts. That's the real life-threatening danger!

The first and most important item to consider for your kits is simply clean water. If you were to create your grab-n-go kit with just a few liters of bottled water, a good water filter, and a few cans of chili, you can live on that! Anyone can prepare at least that little!

Here are a few rules to consider when getting your emergency water in place:

1. **Have the right amount of water.** Usually, you'll want 1 gallon (about 4 liters) of water per person/per day in your kits for drinking, cooking, first aid, and hygiene. But,

because 3 gallons is too much for most people to carry, here's what I do instead:

   a. Pack a total of 3-4 liters of water (about 1 gallon) inside each emergency kit ONLY for <u>drinking</u> to survive 72 hours.
   b. Buy a good water filter so you can create *extra* clean water on the spot for cooking and for first aid, if needed.
   c. Pack away and carry some soap with you so you can bathe in nearby water (filtered or not) that is clear and safe enough to wash in.

2. **Never package or bottle your own water!** Buy filtered, sterilized, pre-packaged water. This will help limit bacteria growth while it's stored in your kits. Here are some different options:

   a. **Pouched Water** – These are typically packaged to last at least 5 years, but some brands may not last that long if stored in the heat (like a car or garage), even though some people claim they will. The positives of this option are that pouches are good for rationing water, since each pouch contains a small portion of water, and also the pouches are easily disposed of. The negatives are that pouches can puncture and can leak too easily in your kits, and they can get quite pricey ounce per ounce when you consider a gallon (3.79 liters) of water in pouches might cost you $15+ U.S. Dollars.

   b. **Canned Water** – I'm not a fan of the different canned water options in the preparedness industry these days, and here's why....

Companies today claiming their canned water will last 30-50 years on a shelf are trying to mimic water canned for the U.S. military around 1950. Those cans used tin or zinc to make sure they didn't rust, but we don't do that anymore.

Today, steel cans are lined with food-grade coatings, yet the residual oxygen inside causes rust and critical failure within 10 years in storage. Also, having seams at the bottom of steel cans develop weak points and leaking over time.

Aluminum cans, on the other hand, even though they don't rust (a lot like tin), are so weakly built, that they require gas pressures (like CO_2 or Nitrogen) on the inside pushing out. This pressure eventually pushes on the seams at the top of the cans, and water will eventually escape and evaporate.

You can go on Ebay on almost any given day and put "unopened soda cans" and you will notice that many of them, even 10-15 years old will say "never opened, but completely empty inside." That's how weak aluminum soda cans are.

I personally stay far away from all cans for my emergency supply these days. Besides bending and breaking-open easily, they were never meant to be stored for 30-50 years, especially with water.

Manufacturers love cans because they're inexpensive to produce and they help increase profit margins, but they're the wrong thing for your emergency supply.

c. **Bottled Water (from the supermarket)** – This is one of my two favorite types of water I like to use for home, work, school, or vehicle emergency kits. (I'll tell you about my other favorite water on the next page.)

Some of the reasons I like bottled water from the supermarket include easy to get, inexpensive, convenient, durable, and versatile.

First, you can simply get these bottles locally at your supermarket and they're really inexpensive and convenient. They're easy to replace every year.

I recommend replacing them yearly because water evaporates out of the bottle or goes bad with bacteria or leaching. (Plastics are porous. Keep your bottles away from chemicals and off concrete because the thin layer of plastic will allow toxins, tastes, and smells to penetrate.)

Next, plastic bottles are compact and quite sturdy and can take a lot more beating and poking than emergency water pouches. Just remember to keep them away from sharp objects inside your kits that might puncture the bottles.

Finally, in an emergency situation, water bottles are quite versatile. After you drink the water in your bottles, you can refill them with clean water, carry them around, and keep reusing the bottles, like a small canteen.

Also, if you run out of *clean* water and don't have a filter handy, you can refill your bottles with water from a river or stream and use ultra-violet light from the sun to kill bacteria and make it drinkable. The Solar Disinfection (SODIS) method is recommended by the World Health Organization (WHO) in developing countries.

To properly use the SODIS method, you'll want to buy bottled water with the number "1" recycle code underneath, and make sure the plastic is as clear as possible with few bumps and ridges, and no plastic-bottle coloring (like blue).

Try to limit the width of your bottles to 4 inches or less—the skinnier the better. The effects of UV diminish the deeper the water it goes through. At 4 inches (10 centimeters), UV-A is reduced to 50%. You'll want the sun's UV rays as strong possible to kill all the microbes inside the water, and that means less depth and more surface area (place your bottles sideways in the sun, for example).

To use SODIS, refill your bottle most of the way with water, replace the lid, shake the bottle to add oxygen to the water, and then fill the bottle the rest of the way up. Remove the label and lay the bottle on its side in direct sunlight for at least 6-10 hours before drinking (or up to 2 days if it's quite cloudy). If you place your bottle(s) on aluminum foil or reflective metal (like a metal roof), the SODIS method works even faster.

You can use glass bottles or jars if needed, yet plastic bottles are the preferred choice because some glass bottles are able to block some of the UV rays that can kill the pathogens. Also, make sure your bottles have air-tight lids.

Lastly, it's important to drink the water or use it quickly after using the SODIS method since any remaining bacteria can multiply and regrow overnight in the dark when the sun's UVs aren't working against them.

d. **Puravai Water** – Another favorite water I use in my emergency kits (besides bottled water from the supermarket) is Puravai Water (www.Puravai.com).

Puravai is the water that government, military, and fortune 500 companies put in their kits. It's a bit more expensive, but it is the best pre-packaged emergency storage water in the preparedness market. Here are some reasons why:

Proven 20-Year Shelf Life – Puravai is the only company I know of that actually has real tests to prove their water will last 20 years or more. The other companies I've researched make 30 to 100-year shelf-life claims, but don't have the lab tests to prove their claims. Puravai does!

Great Value – Since you can store Puravai for 20 years, you don't need to remember to rotate your water. Since you don't need to rotate your water yearly, it pays for itself in a few short years. You also save a lot of money when you consider how water costs increase more each year because of inflation.

100% Bacteria Free – Other water companies in the emergency preparedness market sometimes do the minimums to pass FDA requirements (which aren't very difficult to pass). For example, the FDA doesn't regulate how much heterotrophic bacteria is in bottled water. A company can claim they are "pure" and still be filled with lots of bacteria according to government standards.

Puravai is the only emergency water company that is certified 100% bacteria free. Puravai has even passed stringent Class II medical-grade testing which means it's clean enough for drinking water AND to wash wounds and much more during an emergency, even in a hospital setting.

Extremely Tough – No other packaged emergency storage water can compare to Puravai. Aluminum cans can leak over time, steel cans can rust, and other packaging can puncture, tear, or crush, but thick, BPA-free, high-density bottles can literally last 100 or more years without deteriorating. Puravai is built for the unpredictability of emergency situations. You can drop, scrape, or bump Puravai bottles, and your water stays protected.

Triple Sealed – Puravai bottles have 3 levels of protection: an induction seal (that hermetically seals the bottle to keep your water from evaporating out and bacteria from getting in), a click tight lid (which keeps toxins from getting to the edge of the bottle where your lips touch the bottle), and a shrink wrap over the lid (to make sure your water hasn't been tampered with).

<u>HDPE Plastic Bottles</u> – HDPE plastic is probably the safest food-grade plastic in the world. It's the same plastic used for milk jugs and many of the fruit juices you find in the supermarket. The military uses HDPE for their canteens, and preppers around the world use HDPE water tanks to store their water. You've probably seen the blue 55-gallon barrels that have been used for decades for emergency water storage by many families. That's HDPE plastic!

<u>Floats</u> – Even filled to the brim, Puravai bottles are made to float in any water. You never have to worry about losing your water in floods or dropping your water off the side of a rescue boat and having it sink.

<u>No Rotting/Rusting</u> – Because Puravai uses HDPE bottles, you don't have to worry about mildew, mold, or rust forming and ruining your water supply. Because Puravai bottles don't rust or rot, your water is protected against something as simple as broken pipes in a basement or even humidity in the air.

<u>Reusable Canteen</u> – Similar to the U.S. military canteens, Puravai bottles have a lid that can be screwed on and off. You can carry your water with you during an emergency, drink portions of it throughout the day, and refill your bottle again and again, if needed.

<u>100% Recyclable</u> – HDPE (#2) bottles are able to be recycled completely. Instead of overwhelming landfills, they can get repurposed continuously.

3. **Store the water at the proper temperature.** I like to put my emergency kits in locations that I know won't freeze during the winter or get too hot in the summer. Freezing temperatures can damage bottles (or pouches) as the water freezes and expands, or if it heats up too much, the shelf life of water might diminish.

4. **Think about the needs of children.** Since water is heavy for young children to carry, you can disperse their water supply among the adults or older children.

5. **Buy a good water filter.** You can never have enough water in a crisis. A good water filter (or an easy way to chemically purify or boil water) is a priority in your 3 days of survival. I recommend every kit have a good water filter or filtering system in it. There are a lot to choose from. I prefer electro-adduction filters like Sagan Life or Aquamira.

6. **Have a container to carry water in.** During an emergency, you may need to move from place to place, and you'll want to bring water with you. Make sure you have a water bladder or reusable bottle or another container you can refill and carry with you.

7. **Pack your water so it won't puncture.** Your emergency water is one of the most precious items for your emergency preparedness. Make sure you pack your water in a way that it won't get punctured by sharp objects or get contaminated.

8. **Keep your pets in mind.** Pets are a little more resourceful and resilient than we are, but as part of your planning, consider your pets and their water needs.

Decide on the type of water, quantities, filters, and containers for your kits:

☐ **Home Kits:** _____

☐ **Work Kits:** _____

☐ **School Kits:** _____

☐ **Car Kits:** _____

72 HOURS OF FOOD

The second priority in preparing your emergency kits is having 3 days' worth of food in your packs. Since there are thousands of items you can choose from to get this done, rather than telling you exactly what foods to pick, I'll give you some principles and guidelines and a few suggestions instead. You can then choose what makes the most sense for you and your family.

Here are 10 rules that'll help you pick and pack the right foods, the very first time:

1. **Pack foods you enjoy.** I remember the first 72-hour kit I created. I filled it with coast guard type emergency food bars (e.g., SOS, Mainstay, MayDay, Datrex), and I thought I was so smart until I tried to test them out and actually eat them for a day. I ended up feeling weak and sick in the end. They are filled with calories but very little nutrition, and they taste awful. I think trying to live off those for 3 days would cause me more stress in an already stressful situation. Today, I put food into my kits that are healthy, enjoyable, and easy to transport. I recommend you do the same.

2. **Get the right nutrients.** Back to the emergency bars example above, I think the reason I felt sick eating them is because there was too much sugar and not enough sustenance. Make sure your food isn't just enjoyable but also that it'll keep you healthy through a crisis. You'll want a good mix of proteins, carbohydrates, and good fats/oils. If you aren't getting the right nutrients, you'll lose energy (not a good thing during an emergency). Don't worry, you can still throw in some sweets as comfort foods. I like to put Jolly Ranchers in my kits and some protein bars. ☺

3. **Limit your sodium.** Pick foods where sodium levels are high enough to help with electrolytes but aren't so high that you get edgy because of increased blood pressure. Too much sodium can make you feel sluggish, worn out, or back up your bowels as your body sucks up water from your intestines to make up for all the salt in your bloodstream. When you're taking in over 2000-3000mg of salt a day, you need to drink a lot more water, and water can be precious in an emergency situation.

4. **Pack 1200 to 2400 calories of food <u>per day</u>**, at a minimum. Most people eat between 1200-2400 calories per day normally, but during an emergency, you need to eat more (and more often) because the stress and strain uses up more energy. Make sure you have enough calories packed.

5. **Pack foods that require NO refrigeration and have good shelf lives.** If this wasn't obvious, I'll make it more obvious. Unless you plan to keep your kits in the refrigerator before <u>and</u> during an emergency situation (which makes no sense), pick foods for your kits that can easily store at room temperature. Packing and storing ham and cheese sandwiches in your kits, for example, is NOT a good idea.

   Choose foods that you don't need to rotate every few months. I like to put foods in my kits that can last <u>at least</u> 1 to 2 years between rotations. Some granolas, for example, are so oily, that they start going rancid within 3-6 months, especially in the heat.

   "Date and Rotate" Note: Before you pack your food, take a permanent marker and write on each food item (or food kit) a rotate and replace date you commit to.

6. **Choose food that requires little or no preparation time.** The last thing you want to do during an emergency is prepare a meal from scratch. Don't waste your time or energy, if possible. For example, pick canned or pouched meals and snacks that you can eat right out of the container or just add water to. It's not fun waiting 30 minutes for your food to cook, especially when you or your children are hungry, and you have very little time, water, or cooking fuel to waste.

7. **Pick sturdy foods for your kits.** Avoid pop-up-and-peel canned foods (like Vienna sausages) because the seals have the potential to bend and break too easily. Avoid potato chip bags that are full of air and can pop open if you put a little weight on them. Find foods packaged in a way that won't open easily under pressure.

8. **Regulate the Temperature.** Heat breaks down food, which might spoil your food before the expiration dates arrive. Also, freezing expands and breaks down your food by crystalizing moisture inside and breaking apart the food and sometimes even the packaging it comes in. Avoid putting your kits in locations which fluctuate between hot and cold extremes. Store them in locations that stay between about 35F and 70F, if possible.

9. **Organize your food.** Some people like to separate food into 3 separate days by calories, nutrition (including sodium levels), and variety. You can use large zip lock bags, or duct tape, or whatever works for you. You can even label them Day 1, Day 2, and Day 3, or Breakfast, Lunch, and Dinner if you want.

10. **Pack according to people's needs.** Remember to pack food for infants and small children and/or pets, when needed. Also, keep in mind allergies, diabetes, tastes, preferences, caloric intake needs, etc.

Here are a few food ideas to consider (many require rotation every 1-2 years):

- ✓ **Snacks** – bagged raw nuts, beef jerky, energy bars, protein bars, granola bars, dehydrated fruits, runner energy gels (goo), Jolly Ranchers, crackers.
- ✓ **Breakfasts** – oatmeal packs, granolas, just add water pancake mix.
- ✓ **Canned Food** – tuna fish, beans, chili, corn, green beans, pineapple, Ensure, baby food, etc. (Remember to have a utility knife or can opener in your kit.)

- ✓ **Emergency Food Bars/Tabs** – Though not my favorite, you can consider putting some Mainstay, Mayday, Daytrex, or SOS coast guard approved bars in your kits. I personally like to use "Survival Tabs" instead because they taste so much better and are filled with lots nutrients and work great, in my opinion, for survival situations.
- ✓ **MRE's (Meals Ready to Eat)** – These can be very tasty and convenient but can be bulky and take up a lot of room in your kits unless you break it down into components. The food is usually quite processed, so your bowels might get backed up a bit. They have about a 3-year shelf life, though some people keep and use them a little longer.
- ✓ **Pouched Meals** – For the last 60 years, Mountain House has been the top freeze-dried meal company in the United States and their pouched food will last 30 years on a shelf. They are one of my favorites. Just make sure you balance the sodium levels in pouched meals with other lower sodium foods in your 72 kit.
- ✓ **Freeze-dried Fruits and Vegetables** – professionally pouched corn, peas, green beans, apples, bananas, peaches, etc. (very light weight, delicious, and nutritious, but often low in calories).
- ✓ **Powdered Drink Mixes** – hot chocolate, Gatorade, other electrolyte powdered drink mixes, Tang, pouched dry milk, etc.
- ✓ **Condiments** – prepackaged mustard, ketchup, syrup, salt, pepper, sugar, etc.

If it helps, walk around a supermarket in order to jog your thoughts, and write down any ideas you get. You can make a list as big or small as you want and then narrow it down later.

Once you have a good idea of what you want, group items into meals and count the calories, the sodium levels, and consider the nutrients to see if you have the right mix for your kits.

Jot down some ideas of the types of food you would like in your kits:

_____

_____

_____

_____

_____

_____

_____

_____

_____

CHOOSE THE OTHER ITEMS YOU'LL WANT IN YOUR KITS

To save you some time, below is a list of possible items you could add to your kits. I've added a few blank lines to each list so you can add some of your own ideas or needs to the lists.

Each item below has a checkbox followed by an "**H**" for Home, a "**W**" for Work/School, and a "**C**" for Car. Put a check by which items you would like to include in each of these different types of kits.

Remember that kits can vary in size and contents. A car kit can be simple, a work kit can be a little more elaborate, and the home kits can be built for 3 days of complete survival, for example.

You don't need to check every box. Make your kits functional and effective, but not so heavy/large, you can't move them. Create kits that will fit the best for the crisis situations you're most worried about.

Shelter

☐H☐W☐C - A Light, Portable Tent

☐H☐W☐C - A Tarp or Large Poncho

☐H☐W☐C - Storm/Emergency Bunker

☐H☐W☐C - _____

Cooking

☐H☐W☐C - Can Opener

☐H☐W☐C - Cooking Utensils (Forks, etc.)

☐H☐W☐C - Small Pot/Pan

☐H☐W☐C - Cup

☐H☐W☐C - Small Stove/Grill

☐H☐W☐C - Fuel

☐H☐W☐C - Aluminum Foil

☐H☐W☐C - Special Knives/Tools

☐H☐W☐C - _____

☐H☐W☐C - _____

Light/Electricity

☐H☐W☐C - Regular Flashlights (& Batteries)

☐H☐W☐C - Solar Flashlights or Lanterns

☐H☐W☐C - Headlamp (& Batteries)

☐H☐W☐C - Glow Sticks

☐H☐W☐C - Solar Chargers

☐H☐W☐C - Fire Starters

☐H☐W☐C - _____

☐H☐W☐C - _____

Communication

☐H☐W☐C - Whistle

☐H☐W☐C - Signaling Mirror

☐H☐W☐C - Red Spray Paint (For Signs)

☐H☐W☐C - Portable Radio (& Batteries)

☐H☐W☐C - 2-Way Radios (Walkie Talkies)

☐H☐W☐C - Wind-Up or Solar Radio

☐H☐W☐C - Flares/Flare Gun

☐H☐W☐C - Pre-Paid Cell Phone & Charger

☐H☐W☐C - Reflectors

☐H☐W☐C - Permanent Markers

☐H☐W☐C - Air (Fog) Horn

☐H☐W☐C - Bells

☐H☐W☐C - Waterproof Notebook/Paper

☐H☐W☐C - _____

☐H☐W☐C - _____

☐H☐W☐C - _____

First-Aid/Medical

□H□W□C - Medical History Records	□H□W□C - Medications (3-7 Day Supply)
□H□W□C - Allergy Medication	□H□W□C - Moleskin
□H□W□C - Tylenol or Pain Reliever	□H□W□C - Medical Gloves
□H□W□C - First-Aid Kit	□H□W□C - Extra Pair of Glasses
□H□W□C - Suture Kit	□H□W□C - Eye Contacts & Saline Solution
□H□W□C - CPR Kit	□H□W□C - Extra Hearing Aids
□H□W□C - Stop the Bleed/Trauma Kit	□H□W□C - Religious or Healing Oils
□H□W□C - First-Aid Booklet	□H□W□C - Lip Balm (Chapstick)
□H□W□C - Bandana/Tourniquet	□H□W□C - _____
□H□W□C - Sun Screen	□H□W□C - _____
□H□W□C - Bug Spray/Insect Repellent	□H□W□C - _____

Heat/Warmth/Clothing

□H□W□C - Magnifying Glass (For Fires)	□H□W□C - Good Socks
□H□W□C - Flint and Steel	□H□W□C - Galoshes
□H□W□C - Waterproof Matches	□H□W□C - Thermal Underwear
□H□W□C - Lighters	□H□W□C - Small Portable Heater
□H□W□C - Quick-Start Fuels	□H□W□C - Hand/Feet Warmers
□H□W□C - Tinder	□H□W□C - Emergency Blankets
□H□W□C - Sleeping Bag	□H□W□C - Emergency Sleeping Bag
□H□W□C - Ground Pad	□H□W□C - Other Blankets
□H□W□C - Poncho/Rain Gear	□H□W□C - _____
□H□W□C - Windbreaker	□H□W□C - _____
□H□W□C - Light, Waterproof Jacket	□H□W□C - _____
□H□W□C - Layers of Clothing	□H□W□C - _____
□H□W□C - Winter Coat	□H□W□C - _____
□H□W□C - Winter Gloves	□H□W□C - _____
□H□W□C - Beanie or Headwear	□H□W□C - _____
□H□W□C - Shemagh	□H□W□C - _____
□H□W□C - Sturdy, Comfortable Shoes/Boots	□H□W□C - _____

Pet Supplies

□H□W□C - Pet Toys	□H□W□C - _____
□H□W□C - Leashes	□H□W□C - _____
□H□W□C - Collars	□H□W□C - _____
□H□W□C - Medications	□H□W□C - _____
□H□W□C - Bowls	□H□W□C - _____
□H□W□C - Pet Food	□H□W□C - _____

Entertainment/Pastimes

□H□W□C - Games (Uno, etc.)
□H□W□C - Crossword Puzzles
□H□W□C - Other Puzzles
□H□W□C - Children's Books
□H□W□C - Scriptures
□H□W□C - Other Reading
□H□W□C - iPod/Music
□H□W□C - Pen and Paper
□H□W□C - Journal
□H□W□C - Electronic Games

□H□W□C - Deck of Cards
□H□W□C - Dice, Jacks, etc.
□H□W□C - Frisbee
□H□W□C - Small Musical Instruments
□H□W□C - Chalk or Crayons
□H□W□C - Coloring Books
□H□W□C - _____
□H□W□C - _____
□H□W□C - _____
□H□W□C - _____

Hygiene/Toiletries

□H□W□C - Toothpaste
□H□W□C - Toothbrush
□H□W□C - Floss/Tooth Picks
□H□W□C - Plastic Bags for a Toilet
□H□W□C - Bucket As a Toilet
□H□W□C - Toilet Paper
□H□W□C - Dish Soap
□H□W□C - Sponges
□H□W□C - Wash Towels
□H□W□C - Bar Soap
□H□W□C - Shampoo
□H□W□C - Feminine Hygiene
□H□W□C - Kleenex Packet
□H□W□C - Deodorant
□H□W□C - Lotion
□H□W□C - Comb
□H□W□C - Hand Sanitizer
□H□W□C - Disinfectants

□H□W□C - Cloth Diapers
□H□W□C - Disposable Diapers
□H□W□C - Hand Wipes/Baby Wipes
□H□W□C - Other Infant Needs
□H□W□C - Change of Underwear
□H□W□C - Change of Clothes
□H□W□C - Makeup
□H□W□C - Trash Bags
□H□W□C - Ziploc Bags
□H□W□C - Shaving Razor
□H□W□C - Cotton Balls/Swabs
□H□W□C - _____
□H□W□C - _____
□H□W□C - _____
□H□W□C - _____
□H□W□C - _____
□H□W□C - _____
□H□W□C - _____

Keepsakes (store on the cloud, on portable drives, &/or waterproof containers)

□H□W□C - Digitized Home Videos
□H□W□C - Digitized Photo Albums
□H□W□C - Digitized Journals
□H□W□C - Portable or Online Drives
□H□W□C - Waterproof Container

□H□W□C - Faraday Pouch/Bag
□H□W□C - _____
□H□W□C - _____
□H□W□C - _____
□H□W□C - _____

Protection/Safety

☐H☐W☐C - Pepper Spray/Mace
☐H☐W☐C - Taser/Stun Gun
☐H☐W☐C - Knife
☐H☐W☐C - Handgun
☐H☐W☐C - Ammunition

☐H☐W☐C - Emergency Phone No. Cards
☐H☐W☐C - Self-Defense Skills & Weapons
☐H☐W☐C - Bright or Reflective Vests
☐H☐W☐C - Whistle or Air (Fog) Horn
☐H☐W☐C - _____

Utility Items

☐H☐W☐C - Duct Tape
☐H☐W☐C - Nylon Cords
☐H☐W☐C - Rope
☐H☐W☐C - Nylon Straps
☐H☐W☐C - Climbing Gear
☐H☐W☐C - Waterproof Stuff Sacks
☐H☐W☐C - Waterproof Containers
☐H☐W☐C - A Good Knife (Very Important)
☐H☐W☐C - Utility Tool (Multi-Purpose Tool)
☐H☐W☐C - Hatchet or Wire Saw
☐H☐W☐C - Ax/Knife Sharpener
☐H☐W☐C - Ear Plugs
☐H☐W☐C - Work Gloves (to Remove Debris)
☐H☐W☐C - Extra House/Car Keys
☐H☐W☐C - A Lock or Locking Device
☐H☐W☐C - Small Shovel

☐H☐W☐C - Wrenches to Turn Off Utilities
☐H☐W☐C - Dust/Gas Mask
☐H☐W☐C - Goggles
☐H☐W☐C - Maps
☐H☐W☐C - Garbage Bags (& Ties)
☐H☐W☐C - Zip Ties (Small or Large)
☐H☐W☐C - Binoculars
☐H☐W☐C - Sewing Kit
☐H☐W☐C - Scissors
☐H☐W☐C - Fanny Pack
☐H☐W☐C - Folded-up Aluminum Foil
☐H☐W☐C - Ziploc Bags
☐H☐W☐C - _____
☐H☐W☐C - _____
☐H☐W☐C - _____
☐H☐W☐C - _____

Survival Books

☐H☐W☐C - Edible Plants Books
☐H☐W☐C - Wilderness Survival Books

☐H☐W☐C - Camping Books
☐H☐W☐C - _____

Copies of Legal Papers (much of this can be digitized and put on a USB drive)

☐H☐W☐C - Driver's Licenses
☐H☐W☐C - Social Security Cards
☐H☐W☐C - Other Identification Cards
☐H☐W☐C - Insurance Policies
☐H☐W☐C - Contracts, Legalities, Trusts
☐H☐W☐C - Power of Attorney
☐H☐W☐C - Medical Needs/Blood Types
☐H☐W☐C - Marriage Certificate
☐H☐W☐C - Photos of House (for Insurance)

☐H☐W☐C - Passports
☐H☐W☐C - Birth Certificates
☐H☐W☐C - Stock Certificates
☐H☐W☐C - Car or Home Deeds
☐H☐W☐C - Wills
☐H☐W☐C - Waterproof Container
☐H☐W☐C - Thumb drive/Portable Drive
☐H☐W☐C - _____
☐H☐W☐C - _____

Finances

☐H☐W☐C - Extra Credit Cards	☐H☐W☐C - Various Coins
☐H☐W☐C - Extra Debit Cards	☐H☐W☐C - Travelers' Checks
☐H☐W☐C - Cash in Smaller Bills	☐H☐W☐C - _____

In-house Preparations (extra precautions needed for safety)

☐H☐W☐C - Fire-Escape Ladders	☐H☐W☐C - _____
☐H☐W☐C - Fire Extinguishers	☐H☐W☐C - _____
☐H☐W☐C - Fire/Waterproof Safe	☐H☐W☐C - _____

JUST FOR CARS Section (Additional Car Emergency Kit Ideas)

☐C - Carrying Case/Duffle Bag	☐C - Several Quarters and Small Bills
☐C - Tire Gauge	☐C - Container to Carry Extra Water
☐C - Rags and/or Other Wipes	☐C - Laminated Copies of Driver's Licenses
☐C - Car Wrenches	☐C - Laminated Copies of Insurance Cards
☐C - Other Tools That Fit Your Car	☐C - Laminated Copies of Medical Needs
☐C - Tough Gloves (Rubber, Leather, etc.)	☐C - Laminated Emergency Contacts
☐C - Jumper Cables	☐C - Other Physical Copies of Information
☐C - Foam Tire Sealant	☐C - Car Fire Extinguisher/Spray Can
☐C - Tow Strap/Tow Rope	☐C - Physical Maps
☐C - Snow Chains	☐C - Car Owner's Manual
☐C - Snow Shovel/Small Shovel	☐C - Gasoline Can/Collapsible Jug
☐C - Windshield Ice Scraper	☐C - Extra Oil
☐C - Puravai Water or Pouched water	☐C - Extra Brake Fluid
☐C - Food That Resists Heat/Cold	☐C - Extra Anti-Freeze
☐C - Powdered Gatorade/Runner's Goo	☐C - Extra Water for Radiator, etc.
☐C - Cans of Chili, Tuna, Peas, etc.	☐C - Replacement Light Bulbs
☐C - Meals Ready to Eat (MREs)	☐C - Replacement Fuses
☐C - Energy Bars or Survival Tabs	☐C - Bungee Cords/Cargo Nets
☐C - Warm Clothes (For If Stranded)	☐C - Appropriate Self-Defense Items
☐C - Wool or Other Blankets	☐C - Appropriate Communication Items
☐C - Comfortable Shoes for Long Distances	☐C - _____
☐C - Portable Tire Pump	☐C - _____
☐C - 3-4 Triangle Reflectors/Flares	☐C - _____
☐C - Markers and Writing Board	☐C - _____
☐C - Bright-Colored Emergency Flag	☐C - _____
☐C - Bright Ponchos/Tarps	☐C - _____
☐C - Cat Litter (Soak Up Oil)	☐C - _____
☐C - Syphon Hose	☐C - _____
☐C - Spare Tire/Jack/Tire Iron	☐C - _____

Now that you've created a good idea of what you would like in your kits, you can either purchase pre-made kits (and modify them) or create your own. Either way, at this point, it's a good idea to take separate pieces of paper and begin to organize by person and/or car what you want in each individualized kit. Not every kit needs every item. You can split up items in different kits, if it makes sense.

Once you know what will go in your individual emergency kits, the next action item is to pick containers (duffle bags, buckets, suitcases, backpacks, etc.). Some people pick their containers first, but this should be the last step since you need to pick the right size/type of container to fit all your supplies, not the other way around.

PICK YOUR 72-HOUR KIT CONTAINERS

Rather than store everything in a cardboard box under your bed, you should have a sturdy and portable container you can pick up quickly and run with if needed. You'll also want a container that's comfortable to carry in case you're forced to travel long distances on foot.

I like to pick durable containers with colors that stand out (like bright orange or red) so I don't confuse them with other backpacks, duffel bags, or buckets. In the rush and confusion of a crisis, grabbing a 5-gallon bucket of paint isn't as enjoyable to you or your family as a bucket of survival food, water, and other supplies. ☺

Here are the 5 most popular choices:

- **School Backpack** – Great for simple 72-hour kits, children, or work emergency kits.
- **Hiking Backpack** – Wonderful for more elaborate 72-hour kits (e.g., home kits).
- **Small Rolling Suitcase** – Good for home or work kits.
- **Duffle Bag** – Good for home, car kits, work/school kits. Some even come with wheels.
- **Sturdy Bucket (with lid and handle)** – A good and inexpensive alternative to a backpack or duffle bag, but may prove difficult to carry long distances, especially if the bucket is heavy. Yet, a bucket can also double up as a place to sit, as a toilet, to dispose of waste, or as a way to transport water back and forth – very versatile.

I like to create and pack my own emergency kits because then I can section off items the way I want to, I know where everything is, and I can personalize my kits for each person in our family. Some people prefer to purchase pre-made kits. In any case, some type of kit is better than no kit at all. Let me give you examples of how I like to do some of my personal kits.

My Fire Kit. In the bedroom, next to my bed, I put a bright, small backpack with minimum supplies inside like extra gloves, a flashlight, a fire retardant blanket, a small metal tool for breaking windows, and some hospital gowns (just in case there isn't time to get dressed in the middle of the night and I don't want to stand outside in my underwear).

Next to my orange fire kit is a fire extinguisher, an escape ladder, and typically a pair of shoes. If I needed to evacuate quickly from a fire (or another sudden emergency situation), I have what I need to do so.

My Home Kits. Our family 72-hour emergency kits are in hiking backpacks and include everything that we need to survive for 3 days outside our home (i.e, tent, sleeping bags, etc.)

If a sudden emergency hits and we need to evacuate quickly, my family goes downstairs, next to our cars, and we grab these more elaborate hiking backpacks full of camping and survival supplies.

But that's not all! There's more!! ☺ Next to those hiking backpacks are 2 bright-orange, five-gallon buckets (with lids on them) that we got from Home Depot. They have _extra_ food, water, toiletries, and other supplies. If there is enough time, after we grab our hiking backpacks, we can grab these buckets to bring along as well.

The buckets are "nice-to-haves," but not essential to bring. We can take or leave the buckets, but if we do bring them, besides the extra supplies, they can be used as chairs, toilets, etc.

My Car Kit. In my car emergency kit, I used to carry a VERY BIG duffle bag wherever I went, but it took up so much space, I got tired of it. It made things difficult when I needed to fit groceries in the back of my car. So, I changed how I did emergency car kits in order to fit my lifestyle and preferences better.

Rather than keeping that big duffle bag in my car and dreading it, I now only keep essential emergency supplies in my car at all times (food, water, extra clothes, a portable radio, jumper cables, a flashlight, and a few other supplies). Furthermore, I fit most of these supplies in the extra space around my spare tire, out of sight.

Rearranging and simplifying my car emergency kit freed up a lot of room. I love it so much more than before, but that doesn't mean those are the only things I carry to prepare for emergencies.

When I'm going on a long trip, especially through the desert or in snowy locations away from the city, I put extra food, extra water, a couple of sleeping bags, a ham radio, chains, and other items in my car that are appropriate for that trip alone. After the trip, I take all the extra supplies out and go back to my simpler set up.

That is what works well for me, but you may prefer a backpack, box, bucket, or duffle bag instead. The bottom line is: figure out what works best for you and your family.

PICK THE RIGHT LOCATION FOR YOUR 72-HOUR KITS

Once your kits are ready, store them in locations that are easily accessible during an emergency. At home, you can put them in each person's room, in a closet or pantry next to the front or back door, or in a garage, for example. At work/school, most people keep them under their desks, in a nearby utility closet, or somewhere nearby. Car kits typically go in the trunk.

Wherever you choose to store your kits, make sure they're easy to get to and evacuate with. Also, store them in a cool and dry place, so your food and water doesn't spoil over time.

Goal 2: Create Your Emergency Plans

You've heard it said, "if you fail to plan, then you plan to fail." Well, the actions taken in the first few minutes of a sudden emergency are so critical that they can be the difference between life and death. A good 72-hour preparation should always be accompanied by a good plan.

Consider each person's needs, including those of little children, the elderly, those with disabilities, and even your pets as you work through the following 10 emergency preparedness-planning steps.

As you consider these 10 planning steps, understand that each different emergency situation typically requires a separate plan.

You'll want to use your notes from the risk assessments you did in PrepStep #1 to figure out how to best plan for each of the disaster scenarios you're preparing for, separately.

Remember to write your plans down and organize them in a way that's easy to understand and follow. This will help you practice them in the future and implement them better when you need it most.

It's a good idea to divide up each emergency plan into 3 sections:

1. What you can do now to get prepared and lower your risks ahead of time.

2. What you, your family, or group will actually do during an emergency situation.

3. What to do after the emergency.

Let's getting planning!

TEN EMERGENCY PREPAREDNESS PLANNING STEPS

1. **Risk Assessment.** The first step to any emergency planning is obviously knowing what you're up against. Unless you really understand what you're preparing for, how can you prepare the right way in the end?

    You began your risk assessment in PrepStep #1 as you learned what to do and not to do in different emergency situations.

    What action items did you recognize you could do today (before a crisis) to minimize your risks if that emergency ever did happen? If you haven't done so yet, write these action items down in your plans, separated by each crisis type. Refer to PrepStep #1.

    Now that you have your to-do lists, set some goals (and delegate if needed) to get these items accomplished as soon as possible. As you finish each item, you lower your risks that much more.

2. **Skills and Knowledge.** Next, look at each crisis situation and determine the types of skills and knowledge you, your family, or your group would need to survive each emergency situation in the short or long-term.

To do so, consider a variety of circumstances in which disasters might take place: seasons of the year (Winter, Spring, Summer, and Fall), daytime and nighttime, stormy or clear weather, and even imagine that all the utilities (like gas, electricity, and water) were disrupted. What types of skills would you need to survive?

Write these on your note sheets. You may find there are skills and knowledge in common with all the emergencies you're preparing for. Pay more attention to these.

Here are some skills and knowledge ideas to help get you started:

- ☐ First-Aid/CPR/Herbal and Natural Medications
- ☐ Local/Community Disaster Plans
- ☐ EMT-Training
- ☐ CERT (Community Emergency Response Teams) Training
- ☐ Hunting (Food Finding and Preparation), Fishing
- ☐ Edible Plants (Finding and Preparing)
- ☐ Wilderness Survival (e.g. Books, a Course)
- ☐ Proactivity/Creativity/Resourcefulness
- ☐ Determination/Will to Live/Tenacity
- ☐ Obtaining Water and Purifying It
- ☐ Hygiene, Sanitation, and Waste Disposal
- ☐ Fire Making and Fuel Sources
- ☐ Fire Safety and Common Sense
- ☐ Dutch Oven and Other Outdoor Cooking
- ☐ Crawling, Rolling, Crouching into a Ball
- ☐ Hiding/Protection/Self-Defense/Offensive Mindset
- ☐ Gun Use and Safety
- ☐ Knife Handling, Sharpening, and Safety
- ☐ Communication (Signaling and Sign Making, Whistling, Ham Radio, etc.)
- ☐ Map Reading and Compass Navigation
- ☐ Swimming, Hiking, Climbing, Camping
- ☐ Knot Tying
- ☐ Creating Shelters and Ground Cover for Insulation
- ☐ Animal and Insect Safety
- ☐ Frugality and Making Resources Stretch
- ☐ Turning On/Off Utilities Around the House or Workplace (Gas, Water, Electric)
- ☐ Etc.

3. **Set Rules and Regulations.** Establish day-to-day emergency preparedness rules with your family or group. Pick (or create) a few to implement, write them down, and make them habits. Here are a few examples to consider:

    a. Always have at least ½ a tank of gasoline in your cars at all times.
    b. Always have a pair of comfortable walking shoes, a flashlight, and a change of clothes next to your bed that you can put on in an emergency.
    c. Keep at least $50 in small bills and loose change inside your car, purse, or wallet at all times. The smaller the bills, the better. (If all you have during a crisis are $20 bills or higher, guess how much a bottle of water will cost you?! ☺)
    d. Always set a timer with food cooking in the oven. If you need to leave the house, you <u>must</u> turn the oven off first. (Same goes for cooking food on stoves.)
    e. Never leave a lit fireplace unattended if the protection-glass doors are open.

4. **Delegations and Responsibilities.** As part of your emergency plans, create delegations and responsibilities for each type of emergency and know who does what. You can even divide up responsibilities according to each person's talents/knowledge.

    For example, who will shut off the water, if needed? The gas? The electricity? (Make sure everyone knows where each of these 3 shut off switches/valves are located.) Who will fill up bathtubs, sinks, pots, and buckets with water before you lose water pressure? Who will pick up your child from school if you aren't able to do so?

5. **Buddy/Reporting System.** During an emergency, who will check on whom and who will report to whom? Creating a "buddy" system will make each person accountable for someone else and creating a reporting hierarchy will ensure a parent or leader knows everyone is okay. Once you know your immediate family or group is safe, who else will you check up on (maybe even outside your family or group)?

6. **Evacuation Plan.** Plan how each person will safely and quickly exit a home, work, school, or car for each emergency situation. Try to have at least 2 possible routes for escape (so emergency escape ladders may be needed). Use Google Maps if needed.

    Remember as part of your evacuation plans, create clear and easy ways to get to your 72-hour kits and other keepsakes as you escape. Evacuation plans can be different for each separate emergency type. Write them down.

7. **Where to Meet.** When an emergency strikes, your family or group may, or may not, all be in the same location.

    Whether you're all together or not, you should create places to meet so that you know everyone is safe. (Remember, during a crisis, phone lines are often down or congested, so this step may really come in handy.)

    Typically, you'll want to create at least 2 to 3 meet-up locations, just in case the first location isn't accessible or too dangerous to get to.

For example, inside your home (or right outside your house in the case of a fire, etc.) can be your primary location. But if that's not safe, you may need a second location that can be in or outside your neighborhood (e.g., a church, school, or park), and even a third location outside of town (e.g., a relative's house).

Create "where to meet" plans for each different emergency situation now.

8. **Who to Call/Contact?** Rather than make 5 or 10 calls to different family members when phone lines may not be functioning well, decide on a common contact person (or two) out of town that each family or group member can call, text, or email.

   For example, each person will contact Uncle Joe first. If he can't be reached, then each person will contact Aunt Barbara instead. When you each call your contact person(s), report to them who you are, where you are, and how you're doing.

   Note: If you have a large group and need to reach or warn everyone quickly, you can consider creating a phone tree, where you call 2 people and they call 2 people, etc. until everyone is contacted and reported on. This allows you to distribute or receive information quickly without redundancy or placing the burden on one person.

9. **Emergency Information.** Create and laminate emergency sheets (for the fridge, 72-hour kits, etc.) or small wallet cards for each person that has numbers, websites, and emails of people (or places) to contact in an emergency.

   You can include your common contact person, hospitals, emergency rooms, doctors, neighbors, fire or police stations, poison control, 9-1-1, work or school information, etc.

   You can list all your family members, their dates of birth, and medical information, and you can even include a photo of each person to help search parties find loved ones.

   (On the following pages, I've included example information sheets and cards from www.Ready.gov.)

10. **Prepare Your Plans.** With all the information you've compiled above, you're now ready to begin organizing your 72-hour emergency plans in a way that's easy to follow and practice.

    Organize each plan in a way that you can easily refer to them and follow them. Sometimes the simpler, the better.

    As you begin writing your plans, don't worry if some of your emergency plans feel incomplete or unorganized. As you continue through the rest of the 7 Prep Steps, you'll get more ideas on how to streamline them.

    Once you feel like your plans are pretty solid, you can laminate them and keep them in 2-3 handy and memorable locations, such as on your refrigerator, in your 72-hour kits, in a car, in a desk at work or school, etc.

Family Emergency Plan

Prepare. Plan. Stay Informed. ®

 FEMA

Make sure your family has a plan in case of an emergency. Before an emergency happens, sit down together and decide how you will get in contact with each other, where you will go and what you will do in an emergency. Keep a copy of this plan in your emergency supply kit or another safe place where you can access it in the event of a disaster.

Out-of-Town Contact Name: _____   Telephone Number: _____

Email: _____

Neighborhood Meeting Place: _____   Telephone Number: _____

Regional Meeting Place: _____   Telephone Number: _____

Evacuation Location: _____   Telephone Number: _____

Fill out the following information for each family member and keep it up to date.

Name: _____   Social Security Number: _____
Date of Birth: _____   Important Medical Information: _____

Name: _____   Social Security Number: _____
Date of Birth: _____   Important Medical Information: _____

Name: _____   Social Security Number: _____
Date of Birth: _____   Important Medical Information: _____

Name: _____   Social Security Number: _____
Date of Birth: _____   Important Medical Information: _____

Name: _____   Social Security Number: _____
Date of Birth: _____   Important Medical Information: _____

Name: _____   Social Security Number: _____
Date of Birth: _____   Important Medical Information: _____

Write down where your family spends the most time: work, school and other places you frequent. Schools, daycare providers, workplaces and apartment buildings should all have site-specific emergency plans that you and your family need to know about.

Work Location One	School Location One
Address:	Address:
Phone Number:	Phone Number:
Evacuation Location:	Evacuation Location:
Work Location Two	**School Location Two**
Address:	Address:
Phone Number:	Phone Number:
Evacuation Location:	Evacuation Location:
Work Location Three	**School Location Three**
Address:	Address:
Phone Number:	Phone Number:
Evacuation Location:	Evacuation Location:
Other place you frequent	**Other place you frequent**
Address:	Address:
Phone Number:	Phone Number:
Evacuation Location:	Evacuation Location:

Important Information	Name	Telephone Number	Policy Number
Doctor(s):			
Other:			
Pharmacist:			
Medical Insurance:			
Homeowners/Rental Insurance:			
Veterinarian/Kennel (for pets):			

Dial 911 for Emergencies

Family Emergency Plan

FEMA

Make sure your family has a plan in case of an emergency. Fill out these cards and give one to each member of your family to make sure they know who to call and where to meet in case of an emergency.

ADDITIONAL IMPORTANT PHONE NUMBERS & INFORMATION:

< FOLD HERE >

Family Emergency Plan

EMERGENCY CONTACT NAME:
TELEPHONE:

OUT-OF-TOWN CONTACT NAME:
TELEPHONE:

NEIGHBORHOOD MEETING PLACE:
TELEPHONE:

OTHER IMPORTANT INFORMATION:

Ready ®

DIAL 911 FOR EMERGENCIES

ADDITIONAL IMPORTANT PHONE NUMBERS & INFORMATION:

Family Emergency Plan

EMERGENCY CONTACT NAME:
TELEPHONE:

OUT-OF-TOWN CONTACT NAME:
TELEPHONE:

NEIGHBORHOOD MEETING PLACE:
TELEPHONE:

OTHER IMPORTANT INFORMATION:

Ready ®

DIAL 911 FOR EMERGENCIES

ADDITIONAL IMPORTANT PHONE NUMBERS & INFORMATION:

< FOLD HERE >

Family Emergency Plan

EMERGENCY CONTACT NAME:
TELEPHONE:

OUT-OF-TOWN CONTACT NAME:
TELEPHONE:

NEIGHBORHOOD MEETING PLACE:
TELEPHONE:

OTHER IMPORTANT INFORMATION:

Ready ®

DIAL 911 FOR EMERGENCIES

ADDITIONAL IMPORTANT PHONE NUMBERS & INFORMATION:

Family Emergency Plan

EMERGENCY CONTACT NAME:
TELEPHONE:

OUT-OF-TOWN CONTACT NAME:
TELEPHONE:

NEIGHBORHOOD MEETING PLACE:
TELEPHONE:

OTHER IMPORTANT INFORMATION:

Ready ®

DIAL 911 FOR EMERGENCIES

COMMUNITY or GROUP PREPARATION BEST PRACTICES

One more thought to your planning: If you're preparing as a group, it's important to survey each member to see what skills each has (electrical, CPR, dentistry, ham radio, etc.) and what tools each has (tractors, pick-up trucks, a dolly, two-way radios, etc.). Compile a list of these skills and resources along with names, emails, addresses, and phone numbers.

This list should then be laminated or put in waterproof containers and given to a handful of community or group leaders to store in their 72-hour emergency kits. This information is crucial in organizing relief forces quickly and effectively during a crisis.

Surprisingly, very few communities or groups will make the effort to do this, but you can't imagine how useful this step is.

EXTRA CREDIT

Take time to research the emergency and evacuation plans at your work, school, and the city or town you live in. If there aren't plans, maybe you can help get something started.

Goal 3: Practice Your Emergency Plans

PRACTICE USING YOUR PLANS

Even if it takes hours to get through the first time, practice your plans until they become second nature. Practice allows you to test, evaluate, and refine your plans, and as you practice, your sessions get faster and easier over time.

As you practice your plans, create a variety of scenarios. Imagine you only have 24 hours to leave town, or maybe only 60 minutes, or 15 minutes, or only 2 minutes. Stage a freezing winter scenario or a blazing hot summer one.

You can pretend you're at work, or school, or it's the middle of the night. Maybe you practice staying put in the house ("bugging-in") with all the utilities shut down indefinitely. You can even practice calling your emergency contact number(s) or pretend to call 9-1-1.

Use your creativity in creating different scenario situations, and as you practice, have different people lead and teach each time so that they will retain the information better.

Also, if you have little children, after you practice your plans with them, quiz them to make sure they understand what to do, and stress that it was a "just-in-case" practice, so they don't go to bed scared. ☺

Amanda Ripley, who wrote *The Unthinkable: Who Survives When Disaster Strikes – and Why* says: "Everything you've given your brain before things go bad matters a great deal. It's just amazing how much better your brain can do with a little bit of information."

PRACTICE CALMLY

During emergencies, everyone has a "disaster personality." Some are proactive and wise, and others freeze up or put themselves in danger trying to save everyone. Some people just run away screaming. ☺ In any case, a little knowledge and a bit of calm practice can actually help you develop the right personalities to act smart, not react, in the actual emergency situation.

Most life-threatening mistakes come from anxiety, rash thinking, and rash actions. People who are able to calmly assess the situation and then calmly and quickly choose appropriate actions, often save many lives, including their own and their loved ones.

As you practice your emergency plans, do so calmly but efficiently, so that in the actual emergency situation the correct life-saving decisions are made in a timely manner.

Typically, the way you practice is the way you perform in the heat of an actual emergency.

We all know that young children and teenagers will find it difficult to not run around and scream as they play "pretend emergency," but after they run out of energy, teach them the value of calmness. Good luck!

PRACTICE OFTEN

You should make it tradition to practice your plans at least once a year as a group (or alone if needed). Repetition is the key, and the more you repeat the right actions, the more likely you'll naturally do the right thing should an emergency actually strike.

Tip: Pick a holiday or significant date that is easily remembered each year and make practicing your plans an expected event on that date each year.

GOALS?

Write down a sudden emergency situation and scenario that concerns you the most in the space below. Now, beginning with this scenario, commit to the goal date you wrote at the beginning of this chapter to do your first emergency plan practice and get it done!

_____

Next, write down a list of 2-3 other emergency situations you find important to practice. Pick goal dates to begin practicing these as well.

_____

_____

_____

_____

PrepStep #3

WATER PREPAREDNESS

"Stocking water reserves and learning how to purify contaminated water should be among your top priorities in preparing for an emergency"
- *Office of Emergency Management*

WATER PREPAREDNESS

In PrepStep #2, we talked about the importance of clean water for the first 72-hours of an emergency. But many emergency situations, such as large hurricanes, tornadoes, earthquakes, or floods can leave a city without clean running water for weeks.

On the other hand, large droughts, a devastating solar flare, warfare, high-altitude nuclear electro-magnetic pulse (HEMP) attacks, bio-terrorism (including poisoning a city's water supply), cyber-attacks, a failed electric grid, or even a large pandemic can leave you without water for months or even years.

If such a situation happened to you, where would you get clean water for yourself and your loved ones? Building your long-term water storage (and knowing how to replenish it) is an essential part of *real* emergency preparedness.

SET YOUR "EMERGENCY WATER PREPAREDNESS" GOAL DATES:

- ✓ Calculate Your Water Needs. (Goal Date: _____)

- ✓ Purchase Containers & Store Your Water (Goal Date: _____)

- ✓ Know How to Collect and Clean Water Long-Term (Goal Date: _____)

Goal 1: Calculate Your Water Needs

HOW MUCH WATER TO STORE

It's unnerving to think that if a sudden emergency cut off utilities, most families can only survive for a few days using the water left in their water heaters and in the back of their toilet tanks. That's their survival water!

When you consider that the average person in the U.S. uses 80-100 gallons per day for drinking, cooking, first-aid, bathing, gardening, waste disposal, and sanitation, the question is: how much water should you store up for emergencies?

Obviously, during an emergency, water will be rationed and used only for essential drinking, cooking, first-aid, and sanitation. With that in mind, you should store 2 gallons (nearly 8 liters) of water per day, per person, and shoot to have at least a 1-3 months' supply on hand. If that is undoable, then at MINIMUM, you should store 1 gallon per day, per person (or 30 gallons per month of water storage, per person).

But don't worry, we aren't talking about storing bottled water from the supermarket. There are easier ways to store that much water. We'll cover this later in the section.

When calculating how much water to store, also keep in mind the following:

- Individual needs vary, depending on age, physical condition, activity, diet, and climate.
- Adolescents, nursing mothers, and ill people might need more water.
- Pets also need clean water.
- Very hot temperatures can double the amount of water needed.
- A medical emergency might require additional water for cleaning and first aid.

Simply stated again, aim to store up 2 gallons (about 8 liters) or more each day, per person, for at least 1-3 months, but NEVER go under 1 gallon per day, per person.

EXERCISE #1

How many people are you storing water for? _____

How many gallons per day/per person would you like to store? _____

How many days of water would you like to store up? _____

Multiply the 3 above to see how much water you'll need to store:

_____ (People) **X** _____ (Gallons Per Day) **X** _____ (Days of Storage) = _____ Gallons.

Congratulations, you've accomplished your first goal of this section, so ✔ it off. ☺

On to the next goal...

Goal 2: Purchase Containers and Store Your Water

HOW TO STORE YOUR WATER

Most families, when thinking about storing hundreds of gallons of water, feel a little overwhelmed. I would too if storing that much water meant buying pallets of bottled water from Costco or Sam's Club and filling up every extra space in my garage, shed, or basement.

Unless you're a corporation, hospital, church, government institution, or other organization that requires handing out bottles of water over the first days of an emergency situation, there are special tanks that make water storage so much easier for you and your family. (I'll talk about these on the next page.)

If you *are* an institution that requires bottles to hand out, I recommend staying away from storing pouched, canned, or carton-boxed waters for long periods of time. They are very costly ounce-for-ounce of water and not as secure as people think they are. I would either rotate yearly traditional water bottles from the store, or better yet, store bottles of Puravai instead.

Puravai works the best since it requires no rotation for 20 years. It quickly pays for itself.

STORING YOUR EMERGENCY WATER IN TANKS

My favorite way to store long-term emergency water for my family is in large tanks that are built specifically to handle long-term water storage.

Once these tanks are purchased, they can save you thousands of dollars in water storage costs over the coming years. But you'll have to know what type of containers to buy, how to clean and prepare the tanks for water, where to store the tanks, and how to prepare the water the right way for long-term storage.

What types of containers?

Some people store emergency water in 3-gallon tanks and others go up to tanks as big as 5000+ gallons. What containers are the best to use? It all depends on your needs and wants and how much water you plan to store. Here are some best practices and guidelines you can follow when choosing the right tank(s) for your family:

1. **Big Enough.** Obviously, when you calculated your water needs in the previous section, you figured out how much water you want to store to protect yourself, your family, or your group. Knowing how many gallons (or liters) of water is the first step in figuring out what size container(s) you want and how many of them you'll need.

    Typically, the smallest size tanks I like to recommend are the 3-gallon tanks specifically made for long-term water storage. But if you're trying to store 100 gallons or more, that's a lot of 3-gallon tanks! There are better ways.

    Tanks come in all sizes and shapes. You can find 3, 5, 15, 30, and 55-gallon tanks on the smaller side and 1500 to 2500-gallon tanks on the larger side. Most families I work with choose tanks between 150-500 gallons of water, because it's the right size to save you money gallon-per-gallon and store enough for your family, but not so big it takes up too much space.

    Also, you'd be surprised how little floor space these larger tanks actually take up. A 500-gallon tank, for example, might only require a 3 to 4-foot diameter of floor storage space, and such a tank might only be about 6 to 7-feet tall. That's A LOT of water in a small area, when you think about it!

    No matter what size tank(s) you choose, you might want to also consider getting 2 tanks, rather than just one. I'll talk about my reasons why a little later (on page 101).

2. **The Right Plastic.** Look for water tanks that are built with high-density polyethylene plastic (HDPE) and are BPA-free (which makes water safe for drinking even when stored in direct sunlight). You want your plastic certified for potable (pure enough to be consumed) water.

3. **Proper UV Rating.** Especially if there's a chance that your tanks may be left in the sun for a time, you'll want to make sure your tanks have a high enough ultra-violet (UV) light rating. For example, a UV8 rating means the plastic won't degrade for 8 years in direct sunlight. It also means that if you store your tanks out of direct sunlight, the tanks can last several times longer.

4. **Dark Colors.** For mold and bacteria to grow in water, they crave light. That's why you see most emergency water tanks come in dark colors, so the light can't get in.

   Blue seems to be the most popular color since blue reminds people of water. Yet if you're concerned about others knowing you have water storage, you can look for other colors, such as grey or black, so the bright blue color doesn't attract so much attention.

   I would try to stay away from lighter colors that allow light to get to the water, yet some people prefer translucent tanks so they can see how much water is left inside without opening the tank. If you go this route, store your tanks in a dark room or at least cover your tanks really well with a tarp or other material so it blocks all the light.

5. **First Generation Bottle/Tank.** Even though plastic seems very dense, it can actually be very porous. Even if you wash a tank really well, it will take a lot of work to eliminate the tastes and smells of whatever was in it previously.

   In the preparedness industry, it's not uncommon to hear stories of families buying used 55-gallon tanks from industrial locations to save money. The problem is that those tanks may have been passed on 2, 3, 4, or 5 times. Who knows if there were toxins stored inside at one time? Those toxins would still most likely be in the plastic and could enter into your water storage and eventually into you.

   In fact, plastic pores can absorb chemicals from the outside of the tank as well. Even if a second-hand tank held no toxins *inside* in the past, if these used tanks were stored near dangerous chemicals, toxins may have absorbed in from the outside.

   If possible, I recommend you purchase first generation (new) tanks, and if they *are* used, then be careful and really understand the history of where those tanks have been.

6. **Sturdy.** You'd be surprised how some of the more popular tanks in the preparedness industry are actually poorly built and quite weak. Sometimes when filled with water, "deflection" occurs, and the tanks dangerously bulge out several inches.

   The bigger the deflection, the bigger chance your tank might burst if something heavy fell on top of it or the tank toppled over during an earthquake, hurricane, tornado, or other disaster. You could instantly lose your precious water supply.

   Just because a tank has a popular brand, looks fancy, or has lots of good reviews, don't trust it. Consider the size, thickness, and shape of the tanks when making your choice.

   The bigger the tank, the thicker the plastic should be, and the more reinforcement the tank will need, including edges, fittings, and quality lids.

Also, shape does matter. A tall oval tank, for example, is not going to be as secure as a perfectly round tank of the same thickness, and a square tank will probably need more reinforcement around it, like industrial IBC totes have.

As one more piece of advice, never store your water in emptied plastic milk jugs, detergent bottles, or cardboard cartons like some people do! They're weak, don't seal well, and contaminate easily.

If you need to store water in smaller containers, 2-liter bottles (at the very least) have a more-sturdy plastic and a tighter-fitting lid. Yet, I would recommend you always try to store your water in 3-gallon or bigger industrial HDPE water tanks.

HOW TO STERILIZE YOUR CONTAINERS BEFORE FILLING THEM

Before you fill up your tanks with clean water, you want to make sure they are free of debris, toxins, and bacteria.

Start by using water mixed with dishwashing soap to clean the inside and outside of the tank, especially if the tanks are used. Next, rinse the tank completely with water until there is no residual soap left inside. If the tank is new, make sure you get any small plastic pieces out.

Afterwards, sanitize the tanks by mixing 1 teaspoon of new, off-the-shelf, non-scented liquid household chlorine bleach to every quart of water and put it into the tank. You want that solution to touch (or coat) and sanitize every part of the inside of your tank, including the lid. That helps kill any residual bacteria before you store water in your tank.

As you roll the tank, make sure you don't damage any fittings on the outside.

Finally, wait at least 10 minutes and then thoroughly rinse the tank with clean water to get the sanitizing solution out. Now you're ready to fill up your tanks with clean emergency water.

HOW TO STORE YOUR WATER PROPERLY

In order to fill and store your water properly, here are 10 rules to follow:

1. **Store Away from Chemicals.** Though water can't get out, chemicals and tastes can often still seep into the plastic and eventually into your water, so don't place your tanks in direct contact or in close proximity to toxic substances, gasoline, oil, paints, household cleaners, toxic vapors, etc.

2. **Don't Store Directly on Concrete.** Since plastic is porous, putting your tanks directly on top of concrete can make your water taste and smell like concrete with time. I suggest you place an untreated sheet of plywood, or other board or metal sheet underneath your water tanks in order to shield your water not only from the concrete underneath, but also from cleaning agents you may use to clean the floor around or next to the tanks.

3. **Cool, Dark Location.** Store your water tanks in a cool (preferably not freezing), dark place, if possible, and/or in a container dark enough to block out light. Light and/or heat can allow algae and bacteria to grow.

4. **Out of Direct Sunlight.** To extend the shelf life of your tanks, keep them out of direct sunlight, if possible. If they need to be outside, remember to cover your tanks with a tarp or something else that will protect them from sun damage.

5. **Prepare for Freezing.** If you store your tanks in a place that might freeze, make sure you leave enough air space at the top of the tanks for the water to expand and not burst the tanks.

6. **Use RV or Other Potable Water Hoses.** Regular garden hoses have oils and dangerous chemicals or can be a nest-bed for bacterial growth. To help make sure your water stays clean as you fill your tanks, only use hoses made for potable drinking water (like for recreational vehicle hoses).

7. **Secure Your Water.** Make sure your water is put in a location where heavy items can't easily fall on top during a catastrophe, and if possible, strap large tanks to the wall if you live in a place susceptible to earthquakes or any other disaster that might topple the tanks over.

8. **Treat the Water.** Treat (purify) your water in a way so it will last until your target date. (You'll learn more about how to treat and prepare your water in the next section.)

9. **Tight Lid.** Make sure your water containers have tight lids on them to keep contaminants, bacteria, and bugs out.

10. **Date Your Water.** Put a "stored date" on the outside of each water container and/or a "target date" to replace the water.

    Most people like to rotate their water once a year, but if you keep your water tanks in dark and cooler locations, and purify your water properly, you can sometimes go 2 or more years between rotations as long as your containers remain airtight.

    Most people don't understand that just by opening up your tank to check your water you can introduce bacteria into the water. Keep your tanks shut until you are ready either to use or to rotate the water.

EXERCISE:

In the spaces below, write down any notes on the types of containers you would like to use for your long-term water storage and where you plan to store them.

_____

_____

PURIFYING (TREATING) YOUR WATER FOR LONG-TERM STORAGE

Once you're ready to store your long-term water, you'll want to make sure the water is free from bacteria that might grow over time and ruin your water supply. It's also called "treating" the water.

Often a city's water supply to your home has been purified sufficiently enough to store for 6-12 months without extra treatment (though some people still like to treat city water to be extra sure). But if you're using water from a well, river, pond, lake, or other untreated source, you'll definitely want to take some extra precautions.

There are so many ways to purify water, including using iodine, ultraviolet light, ozone purifications, or boiling water for 3 minutes, but none of these are very efficient when it comes to storing large amounts of water inside tanks at home.

The three most popular treatment methods for emergency water storage are: sodium hypochlorite (household bleach), calcium hypochlorite (pool shock), or chlorine dioxide. All of these treatments can contain harmful byproducts if not applied correctly, so be careful. Let's talk about each of these.

1. **Bleach/Chlorine (Sodium Hypochlorite).** The most well-known method for treating bulk water for long-term storage is liquid household chlorine bleach, also known as "free chlorine."

   Bleach works well to disinfect your water storage typically within 30 minutes, allowing you to store water for a year or more without rotation. It stops viruses and kills most microorganisms (like bacteria), except for tougher ones, such as Cryptosporidium.

   Because bleach diminishes in potency fairly quickly, make sure to use new bleach from the store when you're ready to treat/purify your storage water. Also, don't use scented bleaches, color-safe bleaches, or bleaches with added cleaners (the plainer, the better).

   When you're ready to fill your tanks, you'll want to add a little water to the bottom of the tank first, and then add the appropriate amount of bleach inside before filling up the rest of the tank. Doing so will ensure the bleach mixes throughout all the water as the tank fills.

   Bleach from the store, typically comes in 2 concentrations: *6% and 8.25% sodium hypochlorite. Use the chart here to determine how much bleach to add to your water (for cloudy water, you might have to double the amount of bleach in the chart).

Volume of Water	Amount of 6% Bleach to Add*	Amount of 8.25% Bleach to Add*
1 quart/liter	2 drops	2 drops
1 gallon	8 drops	6 drops
2 gallons	16 drops (1/4 tsp)	12 drops (1/8 teaspoon)
4 gallons	1/3 teaspoon	1/4 teaspoon
8 gallons	2/3 teaspoon	1/2 teaspoon

Once you've filled your water tanks and treated them with bleach, close them with tight lids. Remember, since chlorine gases off, just opening a tank back up in the future might reintroduce bacteria into the water, so don't open your tanks until you're ready to either use the water or rotate it with new water.

If circumstances require you to treat and drink the water on the spot rather than storing it, add the recommended amount of bleach into your water, stir, and wait 30 minutes before drinking.

There should be a faint chlorine smell to the water. If there isn't a faint smell, then repeat the dosage and let it stand another 15 minutes. If it still doesn't smell of chlorine, discard the water, make sure you aren't using expired bleach, or consider another water source that is less polluted.

Finally, DON'T make the mistake of storing away bleach for future emergencies. Due to its shorter shelf life, it may not be strong enough to work as effectively in as little as 6-12 months. If you would like to store away chlorine for a long time, do so in its solid form: Calcium Hypochlorite.

2. **Calcium Hypochlorite (Pool Shock).** Unlike its cousin Sodium Hypochlorite (household liquid bleach) that loses potency quickly, Calcium Hypochlorite has a shelf life from a couple of years up to a decade, if stored properly.

   Like household bleach, Calcium Hypochlorite destroys a variety of disease-causing organisms including bacteria, yeast, fungus, spores, and viruses. Calcium Hypochlorite can be used not only for treating water but also as a household cleaning solution during emergencies.

   Because Calcium Hypochlorite is an extremely concentrated form of bleach, you need to take extra precautions. It's really strong! It can eat through metals that are simply close by, for example.

   I keep mine stored safely inside a glass mason jar with a hard plastic lid on it, rather than the typical metal lid. I then store that jar in a cool, dry, well-ventilated location, far away from children.

   Just so you understand basic ratios, at a 68% pure concentration, about one teaspoon of Calcium Hypochlorite can treat about 600 gallons of city water. It goes a long way.

   Because it's so concentrated, some people find it more practical to purchase Calcium Hypochlorite tablets designed to treat specific amounts of water per tablet. That helps keep people from carelessly putting too much into their water supply.

3. **Chlorine Dioxide.** Even though it contains the name "chlorine," chlorine dioxide isn't household bleach.

   Chlorine Dioxide is effective against harmful parasites, bacteria, and viruses in drinking water without the need for bleach, iodine, or boiling water. It also doesn't leave your water with the unpleasant after-taste of chlorine or iodine.

For example, laboratory reports show that 10 drops of a good Chlorine Dioxide in 8 ounces of mountain water is effective against Giardia in just three minutes and even kills Cryptosporidium within hours. Hikers love it.

Chlorine dioxide is often used in municipal water treatment plants and for disaster relief worldwide. People use it in third-world countries where untreated water can be a major problem.

The way chlorine dioxide works in by releasing nascent oxygen, which is a strong oxidant and a powerful germicidal agent.

Chlorine Dioxide is one of the most thorough ways to treat water for long-term storage. It helps ensure untreated water is free of harmful microbes. The biggest downside is it can be a little pricey for treating large quantities of water.

STABILIZING (EXTENDING) THE STORED SHELF LIFE OF YOUR WATER

Now that you've cleaned and sanitized your tanks, filled your tanks using safe and clean recreational vehicle (RV) hoses, placed the tanks away from chemicals and off concrete, and your water has been treated correctly for storage, before you close your tanks with airtight lids, there is one more trick to the trade you can use to extend the shelf life: water stabilizers.

Rather than having to rotate your water every year or so, stabilizers can be added to the water ahead of time so you can reach 5 years between rotations.

For example, some people will add a good copper and/or silver solution to the water or even colloidal silver before sealing the tank closed.

Silver has extremely potent antimicrobial properties. It only takes one-part silver for every 100 million parts of water to kill microbes.

Silver-ions can kill microorganisms instantly by blocking their respiratory enzyme systems as well as damaging their DNA and their cell walls. It does all this while having no toxic effect on human DNA or cells.

You probably remember hearing stories of the Wild, Wild West and how people would throw a silver coin in their water to help make it safe to drink. It's because it works.

Copper also inhibits the growth of bacteria and algae with a solution as low one-part copper for every million parts of water.

Copper has proven to have a lot of the same antimicrobial properties as silver, that's why you see copper alloys being used in hospitals and on public door handles. Microbes on copper don't live long.

There are a couple good stabilizer solutions on the market if you do a simple search.

Goal 3: Collecting and Cleaning Water Long-Term

What happens if a crisis continues for not just days, weeks, or months, but for years, and you're left without running water? Where will you get more water when your supply is getting low? How will transport water back to your house? How will you filter and then treat dirty water so you can store it, if needed, or how you can drink it safely on the spot?

WATER COLLECTION

If your city's water supply were disrupted and your water storage was running low, how would you replenish your water supply in the short and long-term? Here are a few ideas:

- Water drained from the hot water tank (remember to turn off the gas).
- Toilets (especially from the flush tank, rather than the bowl).
- If you live in a multi-level house, gravity from water upstairs will allow you to drain faucets or pipes downstairs. Open up a faucet upstairs to allow airflow, then open a faucet or drainpipe downstairs and allow water to drain into a bucket or another container.
- A backyard pool (be careful - high chemical levels could cause diarrhea or kidney damage, so pool water is sometimes better for sanitation than for drinking). You may also want to consider buying a good drip filter that is able to filter out pool water and make it suitable for drinking.
- A nearby river, pond, lake, sewer, stream, or community pool.
- Roof water from a storm drain during rains.
- Collect and melt snow during winter.

If you do need to gather water from a stream, river, pond, or lake, remember to collect the clearest water you can find. Typically, you want to gather water a little below the surface but not so low that you gather sediment instead.

Write down a few ideas of where you could collect additional water (clean or dirty) at your house or nearby in the case of a longer-term crisis:

_____

_____

_____

_____

_____

_____

WATER TRANSPORTATION

If you needed to transport 50-100 gallon of water a week from nearby water sources, how would you do it?

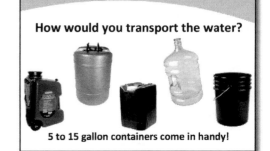

Filling up small pots, pans, and zip-lock bags means lots of tedious trips in order to transport little bits of water at a time. On the flipside, larger containers (like trashcans) become too heavy for convenience (especially if using a car is no longer an option).

You should consider the most convenient way to get your water. If the water is very close, maybe a few hoses and a good pump will do the trick, but, if you need to travel longer distances (especially on foot), how would you get your water back home?

The key is to have containers on hand that are no smaller than 3 gallons (12 liters) and no bigger than about 15 gallons (57 liters). My personal favorite are 5-gallon tanks (like Sampson Stackers), though I also store some 3-gallon tanks (like AquaBricks) and 5-gallon buckets as well. They all come in handy and they're small enough to carry by hand but big enough to avoid multiple unneeded, exhausting trips back and forth from my water sources.

Also, keep in mind that if motor vehicles aren't running, having a good hand wagon, wheel barrel, or bicycle trailer on hand to transport your water will save you a lot of backaches.

PRE-FILTERING DIRTY WATER

Sometimes the only water you can collect is so filled with dirt and sediments that you wonder if it can ever become usable. Dirty water can clog filters, bacteria can hide behind or within different debris, and it isn't pleasant to chew on rocks, dirt, or pieces of wood when you're drinking water. ☺

Unless there are dangerous chemicals in your water supply, most water can be cleaned, no matter how murky.

"Pre-Filtering" allows you to get enough sediments and particulates out of your water so it's clean enough to then filter and treat in a way to make it safe enough for drinking. Many people use the "newspaper method" as a way of determining if the water is clear enough.

To do the newspaper method, put your pre-filtered water into a clear bottle or drinking glass and then place an opened book, newspaper, or magazine on the other side. If you can read through that water, your water is clear enough to further filter and purify for drinking.

Even if it doesn't quite pass the read test but it's clean of the big particulates, you still can go to the next stage of filtering and/or purification using good quality drip filters (which we will cover in the filtering section coming up).

There are different methods you can use to pre-filter (clear up) your water. Here are a few to consider:

Flocculation Pre-Filter

Treatment plants often use flocculation to separate debris out of water. By mixing aluminum sulfate (alum) or ferric sulfate into the murky water, particles clump together and fall to the bottom, allowing you to skim really clear water from the top.

Flocculation can be a little tricky though and mixture ratios can vary depending on how dirty the water is. If you want to test this method out, you can either buy your own alum and do it yourself or use pre-packed systems like "Purifier of Water" from Procter & Gamble (P&G).

Sediment Layer Pre-Filter

Another way to clear out particulates is by creating a *sediment-layer pre-filter* on the spot using items around the house. It may not get rid of everything, but it will serve as a great way to eliminate many of the debris and clean the water enough to treat/purify and then consume.

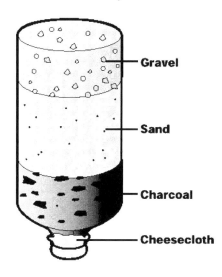

To do so, use a container that allows you to create layers of sediments inside (e.g., a bottomless 2-liter bottle or wide PVC pipe). Seal the bottom with a cloth, cotton balls, or a coffee filter and then add layers of small rocks, gravel, coarse sand, and fine sand.

You can get creative and add more layers of cloth, cotton balls, or coffee filters in between each layer. If you have activated charcoal, you can add a few layers of that as well to help get rid of chemicals and bad tastes.

The idea is to pour dirty water in at the top and have sediment free water come out from the bottom, ready to be treated/purified.

Cloth Pre-Filter

If needed, you can also use rags, a bandana, a towel, or some other cloth from home to pre-filter dirty water. The problem is that most of these have such big pore sizes that the water still comes out quite dirty.

Some people will purchase a Millbank bag or go onto Google or Amazon and purchase polyester felt or polypropylene felt filter cloth to store away in case you need a good prefilter material during an emergency. If you search sump socks, filter socks, or polyester felt filters, you'll find a lot of options.

Ideally you want the pore size to be no bigger than 1 to 5 microns. The water might still come out a little murky but much better than before. Typically, it will be good enough to read or almost read a newspaper through a glass and then you can put your water into a good drip filter that will finish the job.

FILTERING YOUR WATER

EVERY family should have <u>at least</u> one good water filter regardless of whether they have 1 or 5000 gallons of water stored for emergency use.

Drip Filters

I recommend <u>EVERY HOUSEHOLD</u> have a good drip filter. This can become your family's biggest lifesaver. Drip filters use gravity alone to filter several gallons of water at a time, so it saves you time and energy during emergencies. No electricity or hand pumping required.

My favorite two are the Black Berkey and AquaPail (or DuraFlo™) drip filter units. Black Berkey is better at filtering out sediments in the case of murky waters, and AquaPail is more durable than Berkey. Berkey and AquaPail will filter out parasites, bacteria, viruses, and even make pool water drinkable. They can be used as pre-filters, filters, and purifiers all in one, which is very rare in the preparedness industry.

I'm a fan of redundancy, so I own both filters. Both companies back up their filters with more real testing results than their competitors. Each can filter from 550 to 3000 gallons (in ideal circumstances, of course). That's a lot of drinking water before you need to replace each element.

Both systems use candle filters impregnated with silver (which limits microbial growth) and carbon (which filters bad tastes and chemicals).

My drip filters are for ALL my drinking and cooking water during emergencies, even water from my large storage tanks. I'm a fan of being safer than sorry when it comes to something as important as water in an emergency, because a little bad water can do a lot of harm. Besides, putting your stored water through drip filters can help the water taste much better.

Using drip filters with all my stored emergency water means I don't have to worry about rotating my water (though it's still a good practice to rotate). The drip filter will clean the water anyway before I drink or cook with it, even if the water was stored for 1000 years.

Many drip filter units come in stainless steel casings that hold several gallons of water at a time. If those are too expensive, you can create your own drip-filtering system by purchasing your own candle/gravity filters (even from Berkey or DuraFlo™) and two 5-gallon buckets with lids.

To do so, drill a hole in the bottom of the top bucket and screw your candle filter securely into that hole. Then create a matching hole in the lid of the bottom bucket so the stem of the filter can drip water into the bottom bucket when the lid is placed on the bottom bucket.

Now, simply put the dirty water into the top bucket and then clean water will drip into the bucket underneath. Also, the more candle filters you add, the faster the filtered water will flow through to the bottom bucket.

Consider a 2-Tank System

Earlier in this workbook I mentioned that there are some benefits to having 2 water storage tanks rather than just one. Here are some good reasons why you should consider following this recommendation...

First of all, I love redundancies. If one tank were to break, then you have a second tank.

Second, in a long-term survival situation, having at least two tanks allows you to consume the filtered/purified water from one tank while you're refilling a second tank with unpurified water you've collected from a nearby source (prior to purifying it).

Having 2 tanks on hand gives you more options and flexibility without cross contaminating your clean water with harmful bacteria.

Some people like to buy two of the same-size tanks, but that isn't necessary. If you don't need that much water, you can have a large main tank with a smaller one as your backup. For example, I personally have a 500-gallon doorway tank along with a 160-gallon one as my 2nd (or backup) tank.

One More Note About Water Storage

Just so it doesn't surprise you, water that has been sitting in a tank for a long time can taste pretty nasty.

To fix this problem, one solution is to pour the water back and forth between two cups to reintroduce oxygen into the water. A second solution is to have a good drip filter with carbon inside.

Again, Black Berkey or AquaPail (DuraFlo™) drip filters would be my preference in this case.

PrepStep #4
FOOD PREPAREDNESS

"Humor keeps us alive. Humor and food. Don't forget food. You
can go a week without laughing."
- *Joss Wheden*

FOOD PREPAREDNESS

Now that you have your long-term water figured out, let's get to the next big priority in emergency preparedness: food preparedness.

Food is security, and there's a confidence that comes from knowing you have enough food to feed those you care for during a crisis. But getting prepared for emergencies is much more than just buying extra food from the supermarket.

When it comes to food preparedness, there are 4 parts:

1. Short-term Food Storage
2. Long-term Food Storage
3. Long-term Food Replenishment
4. Long-term Food Preparation and Preservation

SHORT-TERM FOOD STORAGE

Building your short-term food storage will probably be the easiest step of all the 7PrepSteps because you're already doing a part of it. You simply need to take what you're currently doing and build a short-term emergency food system around your normal day-to-day routines.

Short-term food storage has a double meaning when it comes to preparedness. First of all, short-term foods are foods you and your family eat each day that you typically store in your pantry, refrigerator, or freezer.

You purchase these foods from your local supermarket or big-box store, and consequently, they have fairly limited shelf lives (usually about 2 years or less). Because they are good only for the "short-term," you're used to buying, eating, and then buying these foods again often.

The second meaning for short-term emergency food storage is that because these are the foods you're used to eating normally, they will also be the foods you'll want to eat for the first few weeks or months of an emergency situation (in the "short-term").

Short-term foods are very different than specialty long-term food supplies (which can sit on a shelf for up to 30 years). We'll cover long-term food storage starting on page 108 of this book.

SET YOUR SHORT-TERM FOOD PREPAREDNESS GOAL DATES:

✓ Create a List of 10 to 30 Day-to-Day Foods You Enjoy. (Goal Date: _____)

✓ Determine How Much Short-Term Food to Store. (Goal Date: _____)

✓ Create a Rotation System. (Goal Date: _____)

Goal 1: Create a List of Day-to-Day Foods You Enjoy

Imagine that a crisis has just hit, the electricity is out, people panic, and all the local grocery stores get emptied out within minutes. When you get there, it's too late, and you hear that relief supplies are at least 3 months out. What are some of the non-perishable foods you wish you could have stocked up on before the crisis happened? What are some nutritious, easy-to-prepare, and enjoyable foods (maybe even some comfort foods) you think you and your family could live on for 1-3 months easily? Make a list of 10-30 of those items:

1. _____

2. _____

3. _____

4. _____

5. _____

6. _____

7. _____

8. _____

9. _____

10. _____

11. _____

12. _____

13. _____

14. _____

15. _____

16. _____

17. _____

18. _____

19. _____

20. _____

21. _____

22. _____

23. _____

24. _____

25. _____

26. _____

27. _____

28. _____

29. _____

30. _____

If you're finding it difficult to come up with 10-30 foods, then walk down each aisle of the supermarket with your family, and you'll come up with a list pretty quickly. (This is a good idea to do anyway!) You'll probably have a bigger list than you know what to do with, and you might have to narrow it down afterward.

The key is to choose foods that you eat on a daily/weekly/monthly basis *anyway*. Obviously, your list won't include *all* the foods your family eats. The goal is to find no less than 10 and no more than 30 for now. (I'll show you what to do with these foods after you've made your list.)

In the meanwhile, if you need more ideas, use the list below. Also, keep your pets in mind as you finalize your food list. I suggest grouping spices and condiments together as *one item* and purchase a good healthy 1 to 2-year supply so you don't have to worry about replenishing them for a while. You're going to use them eventually anyway, so why not?

- Oatmeal
- Canned Chili
- Canned Beans
- Beef Stew
- Canned Corn
- Bag of Beans
- Rice
- Spaghetti & Sauce
- Cereals
- Shelf-Stable Milk
- Pancake Mix
- Syrup
- Wheat Thins
- Popcorn
- Ketchup
- Soups
- Canned Tuna
- Canned Chicken
- Canned Peaches
- Protein Powder
- Tortillas
- Bottled Salsa
- Cream of Wheat
- Honey
- Coconut Oil
- Eggs
- Potatoes
- Peanut Butter
- Jelly
- Granola Bars
- Cake Mixes
- Pudding
- Bottled Water
- Gatorade/Juices
- Mac & Cheese
- Mayonnaise
- Potato Chips
- Flour
- Bread
- Candy Bars
- Food for Pets
- Spices

Now that you have your list built, let's prioritize.

Group "A" Food. Pick the 10 most important items on your list. These are your favorite nutrient-rich foods that require no refrigeration to store and are easy to prepare (with limited or no fuel required). These are foods that can be eaten in small enough portions where no leftovers need to be refrigerated. Some examples could be cans of chili, canned meats, oatmeal, etc. Write an "A" next to these 10 items on your list above.

Group "B" Food. Next, if you have more than 10 items on your list, pick the next ten (#11-20) as your "B" group of food. These foods also don't require refrigeration or can be stored outside the refrigerator until you open them. You can include some snacks (junk food) in this group.

Group "C" Food. Finally, if there are more foods on your list, mark the last group with a "C" in priority. These can even be foods you like to keep in the refrigerator or freezer. If a crisis hit for 1-3 months AND the electricity was running perfectly well, you'd be glad you had them.

As you look over your A, B, and C lists, be realistic, but not too practical. Are these all foods you and your family love and will eat, emergency or not?

Years ago, when I first attempted to create my short-term food storage, I went to the supermarket and bought cases of practically every canned food I could find, especially the foods that I thought were "healthier" and "responsible." I learned two important lessons:

1. I don't like canned collard greens.
2. If you don't buy foods you like to eat, you'll find it *really* difficult to rotate that food in and out every few months.

That's right, I bought A LOT of collard greens, simply because I thought they'd be healthy for me in an emergency. About a year or two later, I attempted to get through my emergency food (I wasn't eating and rotating it like I should have been). I popped open my first of about 100 cans of collard greens, and I took my first bite.

I had no idea how much I didn't like canned collard greens until that moment!

I kept trying to force myself to eat more, and even tried to cook them, flavor them, and mix them with other foods, but in the end, I gave my collard greens to my friend Abe, who is from the South. He got *so* excited, because he *loves* collard greens. Until this day, I'm not sure if it's people from the South that like collard greens or if it was just Abe. ☺

Learn from my mistake. Buy food you really enjoy eating on a daily basis AND aim to make most of those foods at least somewhat nutritious, if possible.

Goal 2: Determine How Much Short-Term Food to Store

Remember, your short-term food storage is a list of "core" items that you keep on hand in case of an emergency. This doesn't mean that it's the *only* food you'll ever buy, so go ahead and keep buying your ice cream and Kit-Kats (but not collard greens, haha). Your short-term food storage is simply a group of food items you'll have on hand AT ALL TIMES.

So, for goal #2, let's figure out your minimums for each food item, starting with your "A" items, then moving to "B" and "C." Your "A" list is the most important, so ALWAYS keep those 10 items stocked up at home, no matter what. And, don't worry, you can refine your "A" list over time if you're unsure. Just get started and you'll learn as you go.

First, decide how long you want your short-term food supply to last. I suggest you store no less than 1 month of food. My personal preference is to have 3 to 6 months of short-term food. They key is to have foods stored up so if a crisis hits, you can comfortably get through it.

Next, starting with your "A" list, create a minimum count for each item for the number of months you are storing food for. For example, you may want 20 cans of beef stew always on hand for a 3-month period of storage. Then do the same with lists "B" and then "C."

You'll eventually put this list on a fridge, pantry door, or somewhere where you can easily review before you go shopping each week.

Here's an example of what I mean:

"A" Foods	"B" Foods	"C" Foods
Peanut Butter (5 Jars)	Wheat Thins (5 Boxes)	Bread (4 loaves)
Jelly (4 Jars)	Pancake Mix (2 Bags)	Eggs (3 dozen)
Shelf Stable Milk (20 Liters)	Coconut Oil (3 Bottles)	Ground Beef (7 lbs)
Cereal (5 Boxes)	Potato Chips (3 Bags)	Cake Mixes (4 boxes)
Dog/Cat Food (2 Bags Each)	Salsa (5 Bottles)	Potatoes (10 lbs)
Canned Tuna (15 Cans)	Rice (3 Bags)	Apple Juice (3 Liters)
Canned Stew (18 Cans)	Protein Powder (2 Jugs)	Refried Beans (8 Cans)
Granola Bars (5 Boxes)	Cream of Wheat (2 Boxes)	Bottled Water (48 ct.)
Instant Oatmeal (3 Boxes)	Syrup (3 Bottles)	
Baby Food (50 Bottles)	Pickles (7 Bottles)	

When you go shopping, the key is to keep MORE on hand of each of these items than your minimums. And prioritize. Even if you fudge on lists "B" and "C," ALWAYS keep up on "A".

For example, before you go shopping, there may be "6" boxes of cereal in your pantry, and you're getting uncomfortably close to your bottom limit of "5" boxes of cereal. So, you probably want to buy another few boxes, because the goal is to NEVER go under "5!"

Keep more than your minimums stored away at all times. You're going to eat that food eventually anyway, so why not get some extra?! Make sense?

Now, if you haven't yet done so, finish your lists and go shopping. Check it off when done:

□ Lists done!   □ Food purchased!

Goal 3: Create a Rotation System

Because most foods from the supermarket can spoil within a couple years, you'll want to rotate the food in a "first bought, first eaten" rotation system. Here are a couple suggestions:

Simple Back-of-the-Line System:

Just like standing in line at the store, the newest person is the one in back. Similarly, a simple, inexpensive way to do your rotations is to put the newest food items at the back (or at the bottom) of your pantry, refrigerator, or freezer.

Rotating Rack Systems:

Though a bit more expensive and can take up more room, there are can/box rotation systems that take care of rotating your food for you. Similar to a vending machine, you load up your food, and the oldest food rolls to the front. When you take that out, the next oldest rolls to the front. You could purchase these systems pre-made, or make them yourself out of wood, plastic, or metal to fit in your pantry, cellar, cupboards, garage, etc.

LONG-TERM FOOD STORAGE

The vast majority of people have only a couple of weeks of food on hand from the supermarket. Now that you've finished your short-term food storage, you should have a system in place that ensures at least 1-3 months of food on hand at all times instead. This way, when other people are rushing to the store during an emergency, you're at home, calm and collected.

But what if an emergency lasts a year or more like a job loss, an economic collapse, an EMP (high-altitude electromagnetic pulse) attack, or a really bad pandemic? How would you survive in the long-term if you've exhausted your short-term foods and you have no way to grow or replenish them? Long-term food preparedness is the answer.

First of all, there's a big difference between short-term and long-term food storage.

Remember, short-term food storage is typically food you buy from your local supermarket and is packaged for short-term use (with a shelf-life usually under 2 years). It's the food you eat every day, and it's the first to be ransacked at the supermarket when disasters strike. It's also the foods you eat on the short-term, usually the first 1-3 months, of any crisis.

Long-term food storage, on the other hand, is comprised of specialty foods that are packaged in a way to last 10-30 years on a shelf without spoiling (worry-free food). This is your food insurance, your last resort food in many cases.

In other words, short-term food storage is usually what you see in your freezer, refrigerator, or cupboard each day, and long-term food storage is what you typically store away in your closet, garage, under a bed or in a basement until you really need it, maybe decades later.

You should plan to store away at least 3-12 months' worth of long-term food storage. It's easier to do than you think.

UNDERSTANDING LONG-TERM FOOD STORAGE

Long-term food storage is one of the most important investments you'll make as you prepare for emergencies. I've seen family after family spend several thousands of dollars into food storage, simply to find out they did it completely wrong, a little too late.

Just a little education about how food manufacturing and storage work will literally save you a ton of money today and a mountain of problems tomorrow (maybe even your life). In this long-term food section, you'll get educated so you don't make the same mistakes others make.

The 5 Myths of Long-Term Food Storage

1. **Living Off Food Storage Is Painful.** In all reality, it could be, but it doesn't have to be. A lot of people think food storage consists of buckets of wheat to grind, or dry milk to endure, but with today's technology, you now have hundreds of foods and meals to choose from.

These days you have options like corn, peas, pineapple, cinnamon apples, stroganoff, lasagna, chili, mozzarella cheese, cheddar cheese, yogurt, milk, beans, rice, real ground beef, chicken, or sausage, and so much more, that will last 20-30 years on a shelf.

2. **Food Storage Is Too Expensive.** There are 2 reasons why this isn't completely true.

   First, it lasts for 10-30 years. That means that if you buy it today and store it away, decades from now, you'll have some pretty inexpensive food, because of inflation.

   Second, it doesn't spoil like that freezer-burned beef in your freezer or that rotting broccoli in your fridge. *That* was expensive food! Haha.

3. **It Needs to be Rotated Often.** Don't confuse short-term with long-term food storage. Since long-term food storage will last often 10-30 years on a shelf, you can store away your food and not worry about it for a long, long, long time.

4. **It Takes Up a Lot of Space.** Most people don't understand how dry and compact long-term food storage is. It typically comes in #10 cans (which is just shy of a gallon in size) and each #10 can holds so much food that you could feed yourself for a month with as little as 6-12 cans of food.

   That can be much more compact than all the pantry and refrigerator space you would typically need to feed yourself for a month. And, it's shelf stable! You can store this food for decades under your bed or in your closet where it doesn't take up much space.

5. **I Can Get All My Long-Term Food Storage from the Grocery Store.** If you're thinking short-term, then you're right. However, long-term food storage is seldom found in local grocery stores. That's because it's a specialty food and is prepared and packaged to stay fresh and healthy for decades on a shelf. Most food in the grocery store expires within 3 years or less.

The 5 Food Killers:

Most preparedness experts talk about the 4 food killers, but in long-term emergency food storage, there are actually 5 food killers, not 4.

These 5 food killers (Oxygen, Water, Light, Heat, and Food Make-up) allow microbes to grow and spoil the food, bug eggs to hatch, food to lose its nutrition, and your food to taste horrible over time. The more you eliminate the 5 food killers, the longer your food will last.

Let's understand each of these 5 food killers and how to limit or eliminate them:

✓ **Oxygen (Food Killer #1).** For long-term food storage, there should be less than 2% residual oxygen left in each container of food (according to military specifications). Special oxygen absorbing packets are used to achieve this. As a comparison, the air we breathe contains roughly 21% oxygen and 78% nitrogen. Nitrogen is good for extending the life of your foods in storage, but oxygen isn't.

Removing and keeping the oxygen out of long-term foods helps keep microbes and bugs from growing and also helps your food taste good years later (e.g. preventing oils from going rancid quicker, etc.).

Some manufacturers claim that a simple nitrogen or CO_2 flush can do the trick and they don't need to invest in costly oxygen absorbers, but that won't work when it comes to long-term food storage that might be eaten decades later.

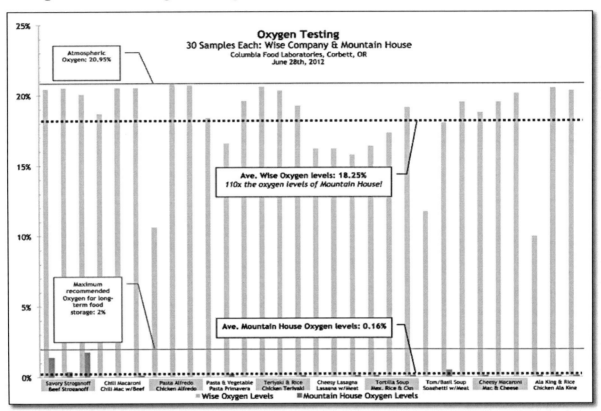

In 2012, Columbia Food Labs conducted an independent study comparing Mountain House pouches (with oxygen absorbers inside) to Wise Food Storage (who used nitrogen flushes instead). The results show that Mountain House averaged less than 1% oxygen, yet Wise Food's averaged over 18% oxygen. What's even more disturbing is many of these pouches measured the normal 21% that we breath on a daily basis.

That would make the 25-year shelf-life claim Wise Food was making, quite a stretch.

✓ **Water/Moisture (Food Killer #2).** Most foods from the supermarket contain a lot of moisture, making them very different from long-term food storage. The more you can limit the moisture, the longer your food will last. That's why dehydrated foods like beef jerky can last a lot longer outside the refrigerator than a sirloin steak can. Even military MREs ("meals ready to eat") need to be rotated every 3 or so years, mainly because of the moisture in them.

We'll talk more about dehydrated (including freeze-dried) foods on the next page.

✓ **Light (Food Killer #3).** When foods are packaged in a way where light can get through, it can cause a lot of problems, especially when it comes to long-term emergency food storage. Bacteria and microbes can reproduce and photodegradation also occurs. That means your foods get discolored, vitamins levels diminish quicker, food spoils, and oils go rancid faster.

✓ **Heat (Food Killer #4).** Obviously, ground beef from the supermarket will last longer in the refrigerator than in your pantry, and it will even last longer in the freezer than the refrigerator. That's because heat encourages the growth of microbes and breaks down food quicker. Eliminate the heat and foods can store longer.

If possible, you should always try to store your long-term food storage at 70°F (21°C) or less but keep it from freezing at the same time.

Because some dehydrated foods still have up to 15-20% moisture in them, when the food freezes at 32°F (0°C), water crystals can form which expand and break down the food. Especially if this happens multiple time, it can ruin your food completely.

As a general rule, I tell people the ideal storage temperature is between about 35-50°F, but since that's not practical for most people, aim to keep it at or under 70°F (21°C).

For every 10-20 degrees you drop in temperature you sometimes can double the shelf life of your food, but on the flipside, for every 10-20 degrees you increase in temperature, you can cut your food storage life in half.

Even leaving your food in a hot garage or shed during the 3 months of a hot summer will wreak havoc on your food.

✓ **Food Make-up (Food Killer #5).** Some long-term foods go bad no matter how good you are at preventing the first 4 food killers.

For example, foods with lots of cooked oils and nuts in them will go rancid faster than foods without oils and nuts in them. Whole grains of wheat will last longer in storage than wheat in a floured (powdered) form. "Component" meals will probably last only a few years, rather than the 25-years most companies in the industry are claiming.

A component meal is a meal that's packaged with a variety of uncooked ingredients inside, mixed together. The more ingredients, the more unpredictable over 25 years.

Unless your meals are precooked and then freeze-dried, you're taking the chance of exponential chemical reactions happening over time. Your food becomes uneatable, possibly even poisonous. Pre-cooking speeds up the chemical reactions ahead of time.

Dehydrated Foods vs. Freeze-Dried Foods

Dehydrated foods are simply foods where the water has been taken out to some degree (just like it sounds), and in the long-term food storage market, the dryer, the better. You usually can tell how dry the food is by how "crispy" (rather than flexible) it is.

Even though freeze-dried foods are technically dehydrated foods, in the emergency market, "dehydrated" and "freeze-dried" are separated by how each is processed to eliminate water.

"Dehydrated foods" are dried out typically using low-level heat, air, sun, smoke, or salt. But "freeze-dried" foods use vacuum chambers and sublimation to dry out your foods. Let me explain what that means...

Prior to freeze-drying, foods are frozen below their "triple point" (the lowest temperature where solids, liquids, and gases can coexist in a food). This is usually between -58°F (-50°C) and -112°F (-80°C) and changes depending on the food.

Once frozen, a vacuum chamber eliminates the water in the food using sublimation – water goes directly from a solid into a gas without turning back into its liquid form first. It's an amazing way to retain the color, taste, look, and nutrients of a food, better than most other preservation methods.

Most fruits and vegetables are dried in their raw (uncooked) state no matter if they are dehydrated or freeze-dried. Yet with pre-made meals (e.g., beef stroganoff, etc.), dehydrated foods typically *are not* pre-cooked. Freeze-dried meals typically *are*. That's really important to know.

As stated before, because cooking accelerates chemical reactions in the food, freeze-dried pre-made meals are much safer and predictable to store long-term. Dehydrated, uncooked "component" meals typically have too many variables and unforeseen chemical reactions inside to predict how long (or short) they will last on a shelf.

When it comes to both dehydrated and freeze-dried food, each has its pros and cons. Let me share with you some of those.

The **PROS** of **DEHYDRATED** Food are:

- **Longer "Opened" Shelf Life.** Dehydrated foods usually condense as they dry. In comparison, freeze-dried foods don't. Since dehydrated foods are so condensed, they rehydrate slower than freeze-dried foods which means they don't spoil as easily from humidity in the air, once opened.

  Where an opened can or pouch of freeze-dried food may need to be eaten within weeks (especially in humid locations), opened containers of dehydrated foods such as beans, rice, pasta, flour, and rolled oats can sit in your pantry opened for years (as long as you don't let critters in, of course).

- **Less Expensive.** Typically, the dehydration process alone is less expensive than freeze-drying. Also, because dehydrated foods are so dense, you can fit more food inside each can or pouch. You get a lot more food for your money.

- **Great Variety.** Since dehydration is a more common practice worldwide than freeze-drying, there is a much bigger variety of food selections.

The **CONS** of DEHYDRATED Food are:

- **Pre-Made Meals Aren't Pre-Cooked.** Unlike freeze-dried meals (such as lasagna, chicken teriyaki, etc.), dehydrated meals aren't typically pre-cooked.

  Dehydrated meals are made up of variety of "component" ingredients (flours, sugars, spices, additives, dried vegetables, quick-cook pastas, etc.) all thrown together into a pouch or can, uncooked. That means the food can ruin sooner due to the chemical reactions we spoke about earlier.

  Also, since dehydrated meals require cooking, they may use up a lot of your precious fuel and time to prepare during an emergency situation.

- **Pre-Made Meal Settling.** Since dehydrated pre-made meals aren't pre-cooked, ingredients like sugar and flour may settle at the bottle while dried fruits, vegetables, meats, and pastas may float to the top.

  That's one big reason why most dehydrated "component meal" companies don't usually sell their foods in #10 cans, only in pouches. Pouches have serving sizes small enough so you don't notice the settling (you can stir and cook all the food at once).

- **Fewer Nutrients.** Because dehydrated foods are dried with heat, air, salt, etc. and not sublimation (like freeze-dried foods), you can lose quite a bit of nutrients in the process (sometimes 40% or more).

- **Rehydrate slower.** Because dehydrated foods are more condensed than freeze-dried foods, they take longer to rehydrate and cook.

- **Shorter "Unopened" Shelf Life.** Certain dehydrated foods have higher moisture levels still in the food (e.g. 5-20%), so while still sealed (un-opened) in cans or pouches, they often spoil quicker than freeze-dried foods.

  And, like I mentioned a few times already, dehydrated "component" meals may not last long on a shelf, no matter how well they are sealed, due to unforeseen chemical reactions in the food over time.

  In defense of dehydrated foods, there are some that are dense and dry enough, that if packaged and stored properly, they can last 30 years on your shelf (like white or parboiled rice, beans, quick oats, wheat kernels, etc.).

- **Condenses Over Time.** Some dehydrated foods actually continued to condense over time. The food is still good to eat but may be much more difficult to cook. For example, after a decade or more in storage, you may have to grind dried pinto or black beans into a powder (or pressure cook them a LONG time), before you can eat them.

- **Weighs More.** Higher moisture and more dense food mean more weight per can of food. It could be difficult to transport from place to place, in an emergency.

The **PROS** of FREEZE-DRIED Food are:

- **Longer "Unopened" Shelf Life.** Freeze dried foods are so low in residual moisture (often 2% or less, if done correctly) that they can store longer un-opened than most dehydrated foods. This low moisture means freeze-dried foods can endure freezing winter temperatures better than foods with higher water content inside.

- **Pre-Made Meals Are Pre-Cooked.** Freeze drying allows for meals (like beef stew or lasagna, etc.) to be pre-cooked and then dried and packaged. Since these meals are pre-cooked, when you're ready to eat, you are able to eat them dry straight out of the can (or pouch), or you can add water and re-hydrate them, if you choose.

  Also, because freeze-dried meals are pre-mixed and cooked ahead of time, powders and other food components don't settle to the bottom of a can like dehydrated, uncooked meals do.

  Note: There are some clever but dishonest companies in the long-term food-storage industry. They will claim "freeze-dried" meals when they're *really* selling dehydrated meals with a few freeze-dried components inside (like freeze-dried corn, peas, or meats). Because it says "just add hot water" doesn't make it a freeze-dried meal.

- **Weighs Less.** Freeze-dried food, after sublimation, is very dry and is extremely light in weight. It can be transported from location to location easier in an emergency.

- **Rehydrate quicker.** Because freeze-dried foods are so porous, they can rehydrate and cook much faster than dehydrated foods.

- **Higher Nutrients.** Since the freeze-drying process deep freezes food and then "gases off" the moisture using sublimation, after it's dry, the food is left virtually unchanged. The result is a super-dry food, often with 90+% of its nutrients (even enzymes) still intact.

- **Appearance and Taste.** Drying by sublimation means the food doesn't shrivel, condense, and darken like dehydrated foods do. The foods retain their appearance, color, and delicious taste over very long periods of time.

The **CONS** of FREEZE-DRIED Food are:

- **Shorter "Opened" Shelf Life.** Since freeze-dried foods don't condense like dehydrated foods do, there are A LOT of pores left in each piece of food (similar to the holes in a dry sponge). Once opened, humidity from the air is able to rehydrate and spoil the food fairly quickly because of these pores. The more humid and closer to sea level (air is denser) you are, the faster opened freeze-dried foods spoil.

  Remember to replace the plastic lids on cans or seal pouches fairly quickly each time you open the container and try to eat your freeze-dried foods within weeks (rather than months or years).

- **Less Food.** Because freeze-dried food is so un-condensed (lots of air pockets) compared to dehydrated foods, less food fits into a pouch or a can.

- **More Expensive.** Since you usually get less food per can or pouch, and because manufacturing freeze-dried foods is often a more expensive process than dehydrating foods, your freeze-dried foods are typically more expensive in the end.

- **More Fragile.** Some freeze-dried foods (like mandarin oranges) are so fragile and light that if the pieces rub against each other, they can break apart and turn much of your food into powder.

Which is Better, Dehydrated or Freeze-Dried?

Which is better for your food storage, dehydrated or freeze-dried food? The answer is <u>BOTH</u>!

Neither freeze-dried nor dehydrated foods require refrigeration which makes each perfect for emergency food storage. Yet, both have their strong and weak points.

For example, when it comes to pre-mixed/pre-made meals, I recommend *only* using freeze-dried rather than dehydrated meals. Freeze-dried meals have a much longer unopened shelf life and retain their appearance, nutrients, and taste better over time.

My favorite company is Mountain House. For over 50 years they have been the premier pre-made, freeze-dried-meal company. In fact, all other emergency *meal* companies (that I'm aware of) can't seem to live up to their 25+ year shelf-life claims, but Mountain House can. In fact, they are the only company that waited 30 years before opening their food to make sure it did last.

When it comes to fruits and vegetables for long-term storage (e.g., pineapple, peaches, cauliflower, broccoli, peas, corn), I also prefer freeze-dried over dehydrated.

Because they are so well dried and preserved, freeze-dried fruits and vegetables retain their nutrients and taste better and can store unopened longer than most dehydrated fruits and vegetables.

I prefer freeze-dried meats for the same reasons. In addition to retaining their nutrients and taste, freeze-dried meats also rehydrate easier which makes them better to cook with.

On the other hand, if I know that I will be opening up a can of food and it will take me months, if not years, to get through it, then I prefer dehydrated foods instead.

For example, individual food components like chopped onion, diced green and red bell peppers, tomato flakes, carrot bits, celery bits, etc., I usually prefer dehydrated. The same goes for rice, beans, potatoes, macaroni, and non-fat milk.

I prefer all these dehydrated (not freeze-dried) because of their long, *opened-on-the-shelf*, shelf life. They can sit in my pantry for an extended period as I use them.

Packaging Types: Cans, Pouches, and Buckets

When it comes to long-term emergency food storage, there are 3 types of packaging that are used most often: cans, pouches, and buckets.

Cans are always the most secure when it comes to long-term food storage, so they're my favorite. The most common can for emergency food storage is the #10-size can (which is just shy of a gallon in size).

Not all cans are alike though. I prefer high-quality metal cans that use a good non-BPA food-grade coating over all parts of the can. This helps keep the cans from rusting on the outside and helps keep the food on the inside from smelling and tasting like metal over time.

Even though cans are the best packaging for long-term food storage and pouches are better for 72-hour kits, there has been a trend in the emergency market over the last decade to use pouches for long-term storage.

Part of this reason is that pouches allow for smaller meal portions to be divided up. But probably the biggest reason is greed. For example, shipping a few rolls of pouch film to a manufacturer is cheaper than shipping a whole truckload of expensive cans with a lot of dead air space. Cheaper packaging means higher profits.

"Mylar pouches" are the buzz these days in the emergency market. These pouches come expensive or cheap, thick or thin, but even some of the best mylar pouches aren't really designed to keep food safe and secure for the 25 years most companies are claiming.

"Mylar" pouches are typically made up of layers such as polyethylene (plastic), porous metalized film, polyester adhesives, etc. Often, it's the plastics (not the metal) that provide most of the protection from the air and moisture. The metalized film is designed to help keep the light out to some extent.

The problem is that mylar pouches still allow light through. If you take a flashlight in a dark room and put it on one side of a layer of mylar, you'll see light come through on the other side. If light can get through, is it possible that moisture and oxygen can also get through given enough time?

To fix this problem, some manufactures (like Mountain House) have set a higher standard by creating a very well-constructed *foil* pouch. Foil doesn't allow light through at all and helps protect against air and moisture transfer at the same time.

In 2015, there was an independent lab study by Fresco System USA where the Water Vapor Transfer Rate (WVTR) of various pouched emergency food manufacturers was examined. (WVTR measures how much moisture—one of the 5 food killers—is able to penetrate packaging over time.)

This study compared the top 3 *backpacker* food companies (Mountain House, AlpineAire, and Backpacker's Pantry) to many of the most popular *long-term emergency food* companies at the time.

Each of the top 3 backpacking food companies had been in business for over 35 years and had a long track record of good manufacturing experience. On the flipside, most of the emergency food companies were just a few years old and were amazing at marketing their new brands but not so much at producing quality long-term emergency food.

The graph below shows how much water could potentially infiltrate the various pouches throughout each manufacturer's "shelf life" claims. The results of the study were a little shocking. This is what they found:

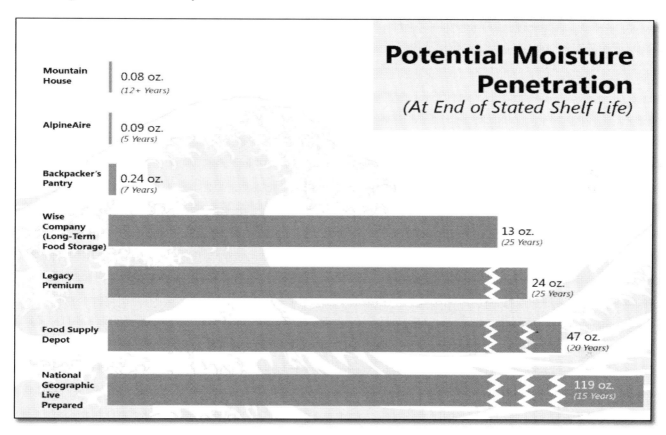

In this study, Mountain House was the only company to use foil pouches (rather than "mylar"), and Mountain House has since tested 30-year old pouches to find the food still in great condition. (Their shelf life for both cans and pouches is now 30 years, not 12 years.)

You'll notice in the study that AlpineAire and Backpacker's Pantry were conservative in their shelf-life claims. From decades of experience, they seemed to understand the limitations of "mylar" pouches when it comes to long-term shelf-life claims.

In comparison, the emergency food companies were claiming 15 to 25-year shelf lives, without proof. Potential water penetration ranging from 13 to 119 ounces is dangerously high, especially for food that may be used in the future for emergency life-or-death situations.

For long-term food, cans are best. Quality foil pouches may also work, but they need to be protected from rodents and accidental punctures. That's where thick plastic buckets can come in handy. Yet because buckets are porous, they don't block oxygen completely. They're better at protecting pouches from mice rather than for storing long-term food for years.

25-Year Shelf Life Claims

The reason food-storage companies can get away with claiming such long shelf lives (when it isn't true), is mainly because federal laws have been pretty relaxed in the past.

For example, the U.S. Department of Agriculture (USDA) writes, "Except for infant formula, product dating is not generally required by Federal regulations. ...There is no uniform or universally accepted system used for food dating in the United States."

And, the U.S. Food and Drug Administration (FDA) explains, "Consumers should be aware that expiration dates are simply 'rules of thumb'... FDA does not require food firms to place 'expired by', 'use by' or 'best before' dates on food products. This information is entirely at the discretion of the manufacturer."

I was speaking at a tradeshow a few years back and when I finished my presentation, I decided to walk around and visit with some of the vendors. I found one claiming a "no-worry 25-year, shelf-life guarantee" on their food. The salesman and I spoke candidly, and he and I both knew that his pancake mix wouldn't last 25 years.

He told me they have a 25-year shelf-life guarantee, and I wanted to know what that meant. He said that if the food goes bad within 25 years, they are willing to replace it for free.

I reiterated that if he and I both knew that it *would* go bad before 25 years, then why not be straight with customers in the first place? It was obvious that as a salesperson, not an owner, he just did what he was told, even if he didn't agree.

The sad thing is what I experienced with that food company isn't uncommon in the emergency preparedness industry. It would surprise you how many companies exaggerate and cut corners in order to increase profit margins.

What's even more disturbing is since these companies *do* cut corners and have larger profit margins, they have the money and the means to out-market their competitors. Bloggers, vloggers, news stations, and families tend to naively believe all the broad marketing exposure and the extensive popularity.

I've been in the emergency market long enough to become skeptical of most marketing claims and to ask the hard questions nobody else is willing to ask. I rarely believe in a brand simply because it's the most popular on YouTube, Facebook, Instagram, or Pinterest.

Just because a mylar-pouch food company claims a 25-year shelf life, or a water-filter company claims 100,000 gallons of use per filter, or a canned-emergency-water company claims a 50-year shelf life, doesn't mean it's true. Companies prey on consumers who simply don't know any better and will believe anything clever marketing tactics lead them to believe.

You'll find that many of the best-quality, most-honest companies can't compete dollar for dollar with the unethical ones, so they're harder to find, but worth it when you do find them. Understanding the principles in this book will help you determine which is which.

Servings, Calories, and Nutrition

When you see companies in the market pushing servings (e.g. "3 Servings a Day!") rather than calories and nutrition, a red flag should rise in your mind. A "serving" of food, for example, may only contain 100 calories or less, so "servings" alone are poor indicators to the value of your food plan.

Most people require between 1200-2400 calories a day to sustain their health, and those calories should come from a variety of foods in order to get the proper nutrients your body needs.

Do a simple Internet search for RMR (resting metabolic rate) calculators. You can easily find out what your absolute minimum calorie intake should be per day.

Calorie Stuffing

Since nutrients are often even more important than calories alone, watch out for a little trick in our industry called "calorie stuffing."

Calorie stuffing is a sneaky practice where vendors add items such as pancake mixes, random soup mixes, oily granolas, or large amounts of sugar drinks into their food plans, in order to "up" the calories. This sometimes leaves your food storage nutritionally un-balanced.

Though certain nut-less granolas and certain fruit-flavored drinks can be good for your supply, large amounts of either are an indication of "calorie stuffing."

Sodium Chloride (Salt) Levels

As you consider proper nutrients, you need to become aware of how much salt is in your food. For long-term food plans, you should keep your daily average of sodium under 2300mg a day.

Some food storage companies ignore this, and when you add up how much salt they supply per 1200 calories, it sometimes gets above 6000mg per day!

High levels of sodium can cause blocked bowels, hypertension, impaired thinking, and the need to drink more of your precious emergency water in order to neutralize the sodium. Statistically, if you're in your 50's or older, it could become lethal.

Now that you're more educated about the ins and outs of food storage, let's get into some action items. Set your long-term food storage goals below, and let's get started...

SET YOUR "LONG-TERM FOOD STORAGE" PREPAREDNESS GOAL DATES:

✓ Decide What Types of Long-Term Foods You Want. (Goal Date: _____)

✓ Choose How Much Food You Want to Store. (Goal Date: _____)

✓ Pick the Right Storage Area. (Goal Date: _____)

Goal 1: Decide What Long-Term Foods You Want

3 GUIDELINES TO PICKING THE RIGHT FOODS

Foods You Love. Like I mentioned earlier, the first rule in picking your long-term storage is to pick foods you enjoy. It'll be difficult for you to endure one week, much less a month or a year, in a stressful emergency situation, if you (and your kids) don't like what you're eating.

Balanced Meals. Next, get the right foods to create balanced, nutritious meals. Just like a good meal would normally include a main course, vegetables, fruits, and other sides, your food storage should be similar.

Purchase no more than about 30-50% pre-made entrees. Though they're convenient and tasty at first, pre-made meals typically have higher sodium levels, so they get more difficult to eat over time as blocked bowels and hypertension set in.

People who purchase only pre-made entrees will wish they had bought more of the staples (like rice, beans, mashed potatoes, fruits, vegetables, quick oats, etc.) after they go a few weeks trying to live off their higher sodium meals.

The Right Mixture. A portion of your foods (usually at least 30%) should be quick-cook or no-cook food items (like quick oats, mashed potato flakes, freeze-dried fruits & vegetables, freeze-dried meats, dehydrated fruits, Mountain House meals, etc.). You never know when cooking-fuel might be difficult to come by in a long-term crisis.

Also remember, if you think it might take your family over a month to get through an opened #10 can of food (about a gallon in size), stick more with dehydrated options for those food items. This will help you protect your food from spoiling from humidity in the air, etc.

PICKING YOUR LONG-TERM FOODS

You can either purchase pre-arranged food packages or create your own food arrangement one item at a time (my favorite way). Either way, it's a good idea to know what types of food you prefer.

To help you along, on the following pages are some suggestions of long-term food options typically available. As we mentioned before, these are foods that are specially prepared and canned for long-term storage. Put check marks by any of the foods that interest you the most, and feel free to add others.

In the parentheses next to each food item is a number that shows roughly how many years each item is able to last (if dried, packaged, and stored properly, that is). Some foods will last more than 25 years, but I've put 25 years as the cap.

Before each check box is a blank space you can use to decide how many cans/pouches of each food you want to purchase. Leave those blank spaces empty for now; we'll use them later.

Note: On the following pages, "MH-FD" stands for Mountain House Freeze-Dried food.

Fruits

___ ☐ Freeze-Dried Banana Slices (25)	___ ☐ Freeze-Dried Mangos (25)
___ ☐ Freeze-Dried Fuji Apple Slices (25)	___ ☐ Freeze-Dried Peach Slices (25)
___ ☐ Freeze-Dried Granny Smith Apples (25)	___ ☐ Freeze-Dried Cherries (25)
___ ☐ Freeze-Dried Cinnamon Apples (25)	___ ☐ Freeze-Dried Grapes (25)
___ ☐ Freeze-Dried Apricot Dices (25)	___ ☐ Dehydrated Apple Chips (25)
___ ☐ Freeze-Dried Strawberry Slices (25)	___ ☐ _____
___ ☐ Freeze-Dried Pineapple Dices (25)	___ ☐ _____
___ ☐ Freeze-Dried Blueberries (25)	___ ☐ _____
___ ☐ Freeze-Dried Raspberries (25)	___ ☐ _____
___ ☐ Freeze-Dried Blackberries (25)	___ ☐ _____
___ ☐ Freeze-Dried Peaches (25)	___ ☐ _____

Vegetables

___ ☐ Freeze-Dried Peas (25)	___ ☐ Dehydrated Sweet Potatoes (20-25)
___ ☐ Freeze-Dried Sweet Corn (25)	___ ☐ Dehydrated Potato Flakes (25)
___ ☐ Freeze-Dried Broccoli Florets (25)	___ ☐ Dehydrated Potato Dices (25)
___ ☐ Freeze-Dried Green Beans (25)	___ ☐ Dehydrated Onion Pieces (20-25)
___ ☐ Freeze-Dried Cauliflower (25)	___ ☐ Dehydrated Broccoli Bits (20-25)
___ ☐ Freeze-Dried Spinach (25)	___ ☐ Dehydrated Celery (20-25)
___ ☐ Freeze-Dried Asparagus (25)	___ ☐ Dehydrated Tomato Flakes (20-25)
___ ☐ Freeze-Dried Butternut Squash (25)	___ ☐ Dehydrated Carrot Dices (20)
___ ☐ Freeze-Dried Tomato Dices (25)	___ ☐ Dehydrated Green/Red Peppers (25)
___ ☐ Freeze-Dried Bell Peppers (25)	___ ☐ _____
___ ☐ Freeze-Dried Onion Dices (25)	___ ☐ _____
___ ☐ Freeze-Dried Kale (25)	___ ☐ _____

Grains/Pastas

___ ☐ Parboiled Rice - Higher Nutrients (25)	___ ☐ Rolled Oats (25)
___ ☐ Long-Grain White Rice (25)	___ ☐ _____
___ ☐ Instant White Rice (25)	___ ☐ _____
___ ☐ Hard Red Wheat (25)	___ ☐ _____
___ ☐ Hard White Wheat (25)	___ ☐ _____
___ ☐ Elbow Macaroni (25)	___ ☐ _____
___ ☐ Hard Corn Kernels (25)	___ ☐ _____

Dairy

___ ☐ Non-Fat Milk (20)   ___ ☐ Freeze-Dried Yogurt Bites (25)
___ ☐ Freeze-Dried Cheddar Cheese (25)   ___ ☐ _____
___ ☐ Freeze-Dried Mozzarella Cheese (25)   ___ ☐ _____
___ ☐ Freeze-Dried Monterey J Cheese (25)   ___ ☐ _____
___ ☐ Freeze-Dried Parmesan Cheese (25)   ___ ☐ _____

Desserts/Sides

___ ☐ MH-FD Ice Cream (2)   ___ ☐ _____
___ ☐ _____   ___ ☐ _____

Cooking Ingredients

___ ☐ White Sugar (25+)   ___ ☐ Soy or Sunflower Lecithin (10+)
___ ☐ Salt (25+)   ___ ☐ _____
___ ☐ Baking Soda (25+)   ___ ☐ _____

Beans/Legumes

___ ☐ Dehydrated Pinto Beans (25)   ___ ☐ Quick-Cook Red Beans (25)
___ ☐ Dehydrated Black Beans (25)   ___ ☐ _____
___ ☐ Dehydrated Small Red Beans (25)   ___ ☐ _____
___ ☐ Quick-Cook Pinto Beans (25)   ___ ☐ _____
___ ☐ Quick-Cook Black Beans (25)   ___ ☐ _____

Breakfast Items

___ ☐ MH-FD Breakfast Skillet (25)   ___ ☐ _____
___ ☐ MH-FD Granola & Blueberries (25)   ___ ☐ _____
___ ☐ MH-FD Scrambled Eggs & Bacon (25)   ___ ☐ _____
___ ☐ MH-FD Spicy Southwest Skillet (25)   ___ ☐ _____
___ ☐ MH-FD Biscuits and Gravy (25)   ___ ☐ _____

Meats

___ ☐ Freeze-Dried Diced Chicken (25)   ___ ☐ Freeze-Dried Shredded Pork (25)
___ ☐ Freeze-Dried Ground Beef (25)   ___ ☐ _____
___ ☐ Freeze-Dried Diced Beef (25)   ___ ☐ _____
___ ☐ Freeze-Dried Shredded Beef (25)   ___ ☐ _____
___ ☐ Freeze-Dried Sausage Crumbles (25)   ___ ☐ _____

Lunch/Dinner Meals

___☐ MH-FD Beef Stew (25)	___☐ MH-FD Lasagna w/ Meat Sauce (25)
___☐ MH-FD Beef Stroganoff (25)	___☐ MH-FD Mexican Rice & Chicken (25)
___☐ MH-FD Chicken Noodle Casserole (25)	___☐ MH-FD Chicken Casserole (25)
___☐ MH-FD Chicken and Dumplings (25)	___☐ MH-FD Turkey Dinner Casserole (25)
___☐ MH-FD Chicken & Mashed Potato (25)	___☐ MH-FD Macaroni & Cheese (25)
___☐ MH-FD Chicken Fajita Bowl (25)	___☐ MH-FD Pasta Primavera (25)
___☐ MH-FD Chicken Fried Rice (25)	___☐ MH-FD Rice and Chicken (25)
___☐ MH-FD Chicken Teriyaki w/ Rice (25)	___☐ MH-FD Spaghetti w/ Meat Sauce (25)
___☐ MH-FD Chili Mac with Beef (25)	___☐ MH-FD Pad Thai with Chicken (25)
___☐ MH-FD Fettuccine Alfredo (25)	___☐ MH-FD Yellow Curry & Chicken (25)

Extras (items not packaged for long-term but compliment your storage)

___☐ Virgin or Extra-Virgin Coconut Oil	___☐ Hand Wheat Grinder (Non-Electric)
___☐ Various Spices	___☐ _____
___☐ Vinegars	___☐ _____

Tip. A good practice when you store your food long-term is to group foods with similar expiration dates together (e.g. 25-year vs. 10-year shelf-life foods). It's easier to remember what you need to use first. You can put the food that will last longer toward the bottom or back of your supply.

It's also smart to use a permanent marker to label the outside of your boxes with "eat by" and/or "replace by" dates. Clearly mark what's in each box so you don't have to open them each time to find out. It will save you A LOT of guesswork in the future.

Goal 2: Choose How Much Food You Want to Store

The next goal is to figure out how much food you want to store. (You'll typically shoot for at least 3-12 months of food storage.)

To begin, answer these 2 questions:

1. How many people are you preparing for? _____

2. How many months are you hoping to be prepared for? _____

Note: As you count the amount of people you're providing for, count little children as if they were adults today, since there's a good chance they won't be children when you might need to use your storage. Even worse, they might be starving teenagers at the time.

Now that you know how many people and how many months of food storage you want, here comes the fun part...

Cans and pouches come in all shapes and sizes, but in the long-term food storage industry, the #10 can is the most common size (and my favorite), so that's what we'll use for the coming exercise. It's just shy of a gallon's worth of food (nearly 4 liters) and 6 cans (a case size) is roughly 5 gallons of food (nearly 20 liters). You can do the same exercise for pouches, if needed.

For now, without complicating things by making you count calories, nutrients, sodium levels, serving sizes, and servings per container, just imagine how much food you, your family, or your group would eat per month of each food item you picked on the previous pages. Don't try to be perfect or over think it. You can adjust amounts up or down later, if you want to.

For example, if you have 3 people in your family and you know you'll eat about 1 can a week of freeze-dried stroganoff (between all 3 of you), then you'll need 4 cans a month. Does that make sense?

In the blank space next to the foods you checked you would write in the number "4." Here's an example:

__4__ MH-FD Beef stroganoff (25)

Once you're finished deciding how much food you want per month, then multiply that number by the number of months you want to be prepared, and that gives you how many cans you need.

For example, if you want 4 cans of stroganoff per month and you want to prepare for 12 months, then you'll want to mark down 48 cans (4x12=48) of stroganoff. You can write the number in the margins next to your monthly counts. It can look like this:

(48) __4__ MH-FD Beef stroganoff (25)

Putting the single monthly count down first (like the "4" above), allows you to adjust the total months (like the 12 months) of storage later, if you need to. You may find out you want 10 months or even 15 months, rather than 12, after you do your calculations.

Since 6 cans come in a case, if you're close to a full case, you may want to up your cans to a multiple of 6. It'll make it easier to organize and track your food in the future. In other words, you would change 17 cans of freeze-dried lasagna to 18 cans (3 full cases of 6).

DOUBLE CHECKING YOUR WORK

After you know what foods you want, it's time to double-check your work. If you choose to do so, then double-check these 3 things: calories, sodium, and nutrients.

Calories

Most every person needs to eat between 1200 and 2400 calories a day of food (if you're an athlete or expend a lot of energy, these numbers might increase).

Keeping caloric needs in mind, add up the total calories for the food storage you're about to purchase and see if your daily average falls between 1200 and 2400 calories per day, per person.

Here's the formula for double-checking to see if you have enough calories:

1. Start by calculating each different food item separately:

Calories per Serving x Total Servings Per Can x Number of Cans = Total Calories (per food). For example, 230 (calories per serving) x 10 (servings per can) x 60 cans = 138,000 calories of stroganoff. It's a bit of work, but it will give you confidence that you actually have enough calories during an emergency situation.

2. You follow the formula above for every different food item and then add all the item totals together, like this:

138,000 calories (stroganoff) + 580,300 calories (rice) + 90,400 calories (corn) + 367,120 calories (quick oats) + 156,000 calories (lasagna) + 110,000 calories (drink mixes) + 310,000 calories (mashed potatoes) + 610,000 calories (black beans) = 2,082,820 calories.

3. Divide that number by the number of days you are storing food for, like this:

2,082,820 calories ÷ 365 days (or 12 months) = 5706 calories per day

4. Then take that number and divide it by the amount of people in your group to get you the average calories per day, per person. For example:

5706 calories per day ÷ 3 people in our family = 1,902 calories per day, per person.

In this example, as long as each person is getting at least 1,200 calories per day, you're doing okay in your long-term food storage plan, but you should still aim for 2400 or more calories per day, per person, if possible (remember, there is no such thing as too much food in a crisis).

Sodium

As you build your food storage, you'll want to keep your sodium levels in check, typically fewer than 2300mg per day, per person. Since I can always add more salt later, I like my long-term storage to have a lot of low-sodium foods in it – foods like rice, potatoes, quick oats, fruits, vegetables, etc.

If you have any doubt that you might be storing up foods that have too much sodium in them, then follow the same formula (above) we used to calculate overall calories and use it to calculate your average sodium intake per person. Just replace "calories" with "sodium."

Nutrients

Lastly, as I mentioned before, make sure that your food has a good balance of nutrients.

Crisis situations can be stressful and to keep yourself from getting sick, you need to be eating healthily. Calories + Proper Nutrients = Sustainable Energy.

Look over your long-term food storage plan. Will you get enough proteins, carbohydrates, etc.? Will you get a good variety of vitamins from the foods you're storing?

There isn't an easy mathematical formula for figuring out a good mix of nutrients, so you'll have to use a bit of common sense.

You can get your carbohydrates from rice, potatoes, quick oats, and even bread you make from grinding wheat kernels, and you can store up beans or freeze-dried meats for protein.

Storing healthy fats is a little more difficult to do for long-term storage. There isn't a great solution that I know of because oils go rancid. You can extend the shelf life of oils somewhat by putting them in glass bottles instead of plastic, and then storing them in cool, dark areas.

Coconut oil seems to do a better job of lasting longer than other oils, but you'll want virgin or extra-virgin coconut oil, instead of refined coconut oil. Coconut oil, when stored properly, can last up to 4-7 years, and maybe more.

Goal 3: Pick the Right Storage Area

People find some of the most creative places to store food - under beds, in closets or basements, and even in bomb shelters, but the rules for storing your food are always the same: Store your food in a cool place, between 35-70°F (2-21°C), if possible, and the colder, the better.

Also, to keep your cans from rusting, keep them dry, and leave your food sealed in boxes, off concrete, away from chemicals, and out of humid locations (or places where water can leak in).

For pouched food, remember to keep it in a container that rodents can't eat through easily.

LONG-TERM FOOD REPLENISHMENT

Where short-term food storage is your first line of defense, long-term food storage is typically your last resort food, if nothing else is left to eat. In between short and long-term food storage is the ability to replenish your food during an emergency, so you hopefully never run low on food. Let's learn how to do that.

SET YOUR "LONG-TERM FOOD REPLENISHMENT" GOAL DATE:

✓ Create a Plan for Long-Term Food Replenishment. (Goal Date: _____)

Create a Plan for Long-Term Food Replenishment

GROWING FRUIT TREES, GARDENING, AND SPROUTING

Being able to grow your own food is the best way to extend your long-term food supply year after year with fresh foods your body craves and likes. Here are some ideas to help you:

Fruit Trees and Vines

If you don't have fruit trees or vines growing nearby that you own or have access to, plant some today!

Fruit trees and vines often take a few years to grow and mature enough to bear fruit, but when they do, you'll enjoy the "fruits" of your labors for years to come.

Plant some grapes, an apple tree, a peach tree, or anything else you really enjoy eating. Even if your yard already has mature landscaping, find a way to make it work.

Fruit trees often require very little work to upkeep once they mature, yet you may want to go on YouTube or the Internet and learn how to prune and nourish them yearly. That will help your trees produce bigger, better, and tastier fruit.

You can also talk to local tree nurseries or agricultural departments at local colleges to learn how to take care of your fruit trees or vines within your local climate. There are plenty of resources to learn from.

Also, don't mind if trees or vines *over* produce since you can bottle or dehydrate the excess, store it away, and live off of it for the rest of the year, each year.

Growing a Garden

If a crisis lasts several months to a year or more (a lifestyle-change crisis) or is big enough (like a national crisis) that shipping and trucking are disrupted for a while, connecting with local farmers or learning how to grow your own garden might someday save your family.

Knowing how to grow, prepare, and even store away your own vegetables are essential skills that will build your confidence in your ability to survive. If you haven't done so yet, then start! Besides, saving $100's in grocery bills each summer is a nice perk to growing a garden.

As you learn how to plant and grow your own vegetables, you can gather seeds each summer for the following year. For example, you can let seeds from tomatoes, squash, or cucumbers dry out and then store them in a cool, dry location. You can even let beans or peas dry out on the vine before collecting them. Or, let some your herbs like onion and parsley keep growing until they form seeds ("go to seed") and dry out naturally. It's pretty fun to learn how to do.

If you aren't doing your own gardening already or have limited space, you can start simply by creating or joining a community or neighborhood garden, finding a little plot in your back or front yard, or building some planters and doing some square-foot gardening.

If you're adventurous or a little more skilled, you can build a greenhouse or a geodesic dome garden and even add hydroponics or aquaponics to your greenhouse.

Again, learn to plant and grow the vegetables or herbs you know you will enjoy eating.

Sprouting

Sprouting is the process of germinating seeds and then eating their "sprouts" either raw or cooked. If you don't know what sprouting is, think "alfalfa sprouts" from the store. You get the seeds growing big enough to eat, but not more than a few inches.

Sprouting is commonly done indoors and requires very little water, which makes sprouting an essential skill to learn for long-term survival. You can easily create a greenhouse *inside* your house with very little space.

Study up on sprouting and you'll be amazed at how powerful it is for your long-term food plan.

With sprouting you can create fresh food even in the dead of winter when vegetable gardens and fruit trees may not be producing. And, you can grow a new "crop" every few days, which gives you a constant supply of proteins, vitamins, and other nutrients.

The first rule, again, is to find sprouts you really enjoy eating. To do so, you should find a supply of organic or non-GMO seeds, learn how each seed best grows, and then test out different types of sprouts until you narrow down the ones that work best for your tastes.

Because different types of sprouts supply different types of nutrients, you may want to learn how to grow several different types of seeds. Here is a partial list to choose from:

- **Pulses (legumes, pea family):** soybean (bean sprouts), alfalfa, mung bean, pea, chickpea, soybean, lentils, clover, fenugreek, etc.
- **Cereals and Pseudocereals:** wheat grass, rice, triticale, barley, rye, maize (corn), quinoa, amaranth, buckwheat, spelt, etc.
- **Brassicas (cabbage family):** cabbage, watercress, mustard, radish, turnip, broccoli, mizuna, etc.
- **Oilseeds:** sesame, sunflower, almond, hazelnut, peanut, etc.
- **Allium (onions):** onion, green onion, leek
- **Green and Microgreens:** milk thistle, lemon grass, carrot, fennel, parsley, spinach, celery, lettuce, etc.

There are several others, but you may want to begin by learning with alfalfa or mung beans to build your confidence. As you master this skill, you can also learn to grow other types of foods indoors, such as herbs, etc., if you choose to do so.

HUNTING AND FISHING

Another way to replenish your food supply is by hunting or fishing. Just remember that depending on the long-term crisis, you may or may not have access to refrigeration. So to preserve your meats longer, you'll need to dehydrate, smoke your meats, or use salt to help extend their shelf life.

Salt is a good preservative because it binds water and helps keep microbes from growing. Make sure you keep a good amount of salt stored away for this purpose alone.

You can also pressure cook your meats in mason jars for longer-term storage. Once opened, unless you have access to refrigeration, plan to eat the full jar of meat in one sitting to avoid bacterial growth.

LIVESTOCK, POULTRY, AND DAIRY

One more piece of advice for long-term food replenishment is to consider getting chickens, ducks, rabbits, goats, pigs, or other livestock. These can provide you with eggs, milk, or meat, if necessary.

FOOD PREPARATION AND PRESERVATION

As you replenish your food supply each year, you'll want to know how to prepare and preserve it for long-term use. I'll give you some ideas on the following pages.

SET YOUR "FOOD PREPARANTION AND PRESERVATION PLAN" GOAL DATE:

Create a Plan for Food Preparation and Preservation. (Goal Date: _____)

Create a Plan for Food Preparation and Preservation

Obviously, it's hard to prepare food without the tools and knowledge to do so in the midst of an emergency. Make sure you're equipped with items you already have around the house and other items you may need to purchase before a crisis takes place. Here are some ideas:

Food Preparation Tools and Supplies Ideas

☐ Zeer-Pot Refrigeration	☐ Utensils
☐ Portable Stoves – Coleman, Volcano, etc.	☐ Extra Can-Openers
☐ Solar Oven	☐ Bowls, Plates, Cups
☐ Barbecue	☐ Disposable Bowls, Plates, and Cups
☐ Fireplace or Fire Pit	☐ Coolers and Ice Packs
☐ Pots, Pans, Pressure Cookers	☐ _____
☐ Dutch Ovens & Supplies	☐ _____
☐ Hand-Crank Wheat Grinder	☐ _____

Canning

One big problem with fruit trees/vines and vegetable gardens is that they usually only produce one or two times a year. That means if you need to replenish your food supply year to year, you need to go one step further and learn how to bottle your food for long-term storage.

"Canning" or "bottling" are terms used for putting food into glass jars and then preparing them for long-term storage (outside the refrigerator) for a year or more. A good long-term-crisis plan involves learning how to can your food, so you make it through the winter months, when food doesn't grow as easily.

Canning works for vegetables, fruits, meats, meals, and so much more. You can store juice from your grapes, salsa from your garden tomatoes, peaches from your fruit trees, jelly from your strawberries, or pickles from your cucumber garden. You can even cook up and bottle your favorite chili recipe and enjoy it year-round.

If you are going to take canning seriously, I recommend buying anywhere from 25 to 100 mason jars and enough lids and rings for each one.

You'll also want to purchase <u>several</u> extra lids (not rings) since you should replace the lids each time you retort (cook up) a new batch of food.

Used lids don't seal as well as new ones because they already have an impression groove in them from the last batch. It's not necessary, but if you want, you can buy up a few extra rings as well, just in case some get damaged.

Some foods from the supermarket come in bottles that are perfect fits for mason jars lids and rings. When I come across these jars, I keep them and add them to my jar storage. You should consider doing the same.

As part of your preparation, purchase a good pressure canner, canning tools, and a good canning book. I'm a fan of the All-American Pressure Canner which requires no rubber gaskets to work, so you won't need replacement parts during a long-term crisis.

I also recommend that you purchase the latest edition of the *Ball Blue Book Guide to Preserving* to make sure you have the most recent canning techniques and information at your fingertips.

Don't take chances at canning without a good manual since some foods are great candidates for botulism, especially if you don't follow the right guidelines or recipes.

Don't mess with botulism!

Dehydrating & Freeze Drying

Another way to preserve your food for the long term is to dehydrate or freeze-dry it yourself. You can use heat/smoke drying (e.g., beef jerky), or sun drying (like with herbs and tomatoes). You can also purchase a home dehydrator to do a variety of foods. I use an Excalibur 9-tray dehydrator because of how much surface area it offers.

There are also home freeze-drying units (like Harvest Right) that allow you to freeze dry almost anything from your favorite meals to cookies and Gummy Bears.

As a little note, once you dehydrate or freeze dry your foods, then follow the food-storage rules you learned in previous sections to extend shelf lives.

For example, you can store your dehydrated foods in airtight mason jars and store them in dark, cool locations until you're ready to use them.

To help you get rid of the oxygen in each mason jar before storing them, you can use oxygen absorbers, but those are difficult to get during a long-term emergency. To get around this problem, you can use a FoodSaver instead.

FoodSaver has a mason jar attachment you can buy online from Amazon and a few other places. The mason jar attachment will suck the air out of the jars before sealing the lid on top.

That is my favorite way of storing foods I dehydrate at home.

PRACTICE YOUR LONG-TERM FOOD PLANS

Finally, from experience, one more important piece of advice is to buy a little extra food storage and try to live off it for a week or more. You'll learn very quickly what works for you and what doesn't, and you might find out there are some foods missing or maybe even some you'd like to replace.

Also, don't wait to learn how to garden, or grow some sprouts, or practice preserving your food. You'll gain the experience and the confidence you and your family need to survive a long-term crisis comfortably.

PrepStep #5
MEET YOUR OTHER NEEDS

"Because you never know when the day before…Is the day before. Prepare for tomorrow."
- Bobby Akart

MEET YOUR OTHER NEEDS

Many of the clients I work with wonder if they can really ever get prepared for all types of emergency situations, and the answer is "yes." To do so, you need to first imagine the worst-case scenarios and create a solid plan on how to survive those scenarios. Then, if anything less catastrophic happens, you'll be more than prepared. Here are some examples of scenarios:

An EMP attack or unexpected solar storm (coronal mass ejection) could leave a country (or several countries) without food production, running water, electricity, gas, communication, transportation, or law-and-order for a year or more.

A massive financial meltdown could cause long-term chaos, riots, and starvation, similar to what happened in Venezuela and Germany. That could mean you need to know how to protect your family and provide for them, possibly even for half a decade or more.

A dangerous worldwide pandemic might leave you isolated in your house for months, if not years, until the danger passes. If it gets really bad, people don't go to work, and that means no supermarkets, restaurants, public services, and maybe even utilities for a while.

A war waged on your country's soil could also cause shortages of food, water, heat, police protection, and more. The more prepared you are at home (or another safe place), the more of a chance you have for survival.

In emergency situations such as those mentioned above, having 72-hour kits, water storage, and short and long-term foods in place is only half the battle. You should also make sure your "other needs" are met.

"Other needs" include being able to heat or cool your house (or yourself), as well as having fuel, alternative light and energy, shelter, first-aid & health supplies, communications, hygiene, sanitation, disposal, transportation, self-defense, safety, entertainment, survival skills, and other needed supplies (or tools) in place.

Since every family has different needs (depending on the type of crisis), the following pages will give you several ideas to choose from in order to help you meet your "other needs" for survival. There are several categories and options to choose from, but feel free to add more to the lists or customize them how you like.

As you find what works for you (or could possibly work for you) under each category, feel free to put check marks next to those ideas you find most useful for your needs.

SET YOUR "OTHER NEEDS" PREPAREDNESS GOAL DATE:

- ✓ Choose Preparedness Items/Skills for Your "Other Needs." (Goal Date: _____)

- ✓ Purchase Those Items or Learn Those Skills. (Goal Date: _____)

Heating and Cooling

To survive extreme cold or heat situations, you need a little bit of planning. If possible, insulate your house well ahead of time. Next, store the proper layers of clothing and bedding to warm yourself (without sweating) or light clothing for the heat. Then, purchase other items you need to protect your family the right way. Remember, don't run typical combustion generators, standard open fires, or BBQs indoors because of carbon monoxide poisoning. Here are some ideas to help you stay warm or cool in an emergency:

Heating/Cooling Ideas – If utilities were cut off, how would you keep warm/cool?

☐ Whole-House Insulation
☐ Weather Stripping
☐ 6mil+ Visqueen or Plastic Sheeting
☐ Reflective Film for Windows
☐ Canopy or Porch Covers
☐ Long Johns and layers of clothing
☐ Insulated Boots
☐ Merino Wool or Synthetic Socks
☐ Winter Coat
☐ Windbreaker
☐ Beanie
☐ Mittens
☐ Gloves
☐ Fleece Pull-Over

☐ Sleeping Bags
☐ Space Heater/Portable-Heating Units
☐ Mr. Heater with Extra Propane Tanks
☐ Wood-Burning Stove/Heater/Furnace
☐ Wood Storage
☐ Hand Warmers
☐ Lighters, Matches, Kindling
☐ Fire Starting/Building/Safety Skills
☐ Fireplace/Rocket Mass/Masonry Heaters
☐ Geo-Thermal/Solar
☐ Portable Fan for Cooling
☐ Loose, Light Weight & Colored Clothes
☐ _____
☐ _____

Fuel

Storing the right types of fuel (and knowing how to produce more) can help you make it comfortably through any short or long-term crisis. Good fuel sources can be used for cooking, warmth, light, and even running various devices. Here are some ideas to help you:

Fuel Ideas – Needed for cooking, warmth, production, and so much more.

☐ Biofuel Creation Skills
☐ Coal or Charcoal
☐ Firewood
☐ Propane Tanks
☐ Matches/Lighters/Fire Starters
☐ Kindling, Lint, Newspaper, Etc.
☐ Methane

☐ Kerosene
☐ Solar Water Heater & Solar Appliances
☐ Gasoline (Short-Term)
☐ Geo-Thermal
☐ _____
☐ _____
☐ _____

Alternative Light and Energy

While natural disasters could knock out power for weeks or months, extreme events, such as electric grid cyber-attacks, EMPs, solar storms, or major pandemics, could leave you without power for years. In worst case scenarios and during long-term emergencies, how will you keep your house lit, see clearly at night, or have electricity for essential appliances?

Solar panels, power banks, kinetic energy devices, or various power generators are all good to consider. I prefer solar since it's quiet and doesn't draw attention to your house in a crisis. Some people prefer combustion generators for the amount of power they produce. If that's you, my suggestion is to get one that runs on propane. Propane can store for more than a decade where gasoline goes bad quickly. Below are some light and energy ideas to consider:

Alternative Light/Energy Ideas – How to make it long term if the power goes out.

- ☐ Energy efficient bulbs and appliances
- ☐ Electric Power Banks
- ☐ Solar, Crank, or Regular Flashlights
- ☐ Supply of Batteries
- ☐ Candles or Oil Lamps
- ☐ Solar Panels
- ☐ Portable Solar Chargers
- ☐ Wind Turbines
- ☐ Hydro-Electric Generators

- ☐ Solar Garden Lights (Use as Lanterns)
- ☐ Roof Skylights
- ☐ Reflective Panels
- ☐ Bio, Propane, or Other Generators
- ☐ _____
- ☐ _____
- ☐ _____
- ☐ _____
- ☐ _____

Shelter

Hopefully during any short-term or long-term crisis, you'll still be able to stay inside your home. But what if you're forced out of your home? That's when shelter preparations done ahead of time will come in handy. Here are a few thoughts to consider:

Shelter Ideas – Protect yourself from heat, cold, elements, animals, and other people.

- ☐ List of Churches, Schools, and Public Places
- ☐ Relative's/Friend's Houses (In the Area)
- ☐ Relative's/Friend's Houses (Out of Area)
- ☐ Camper or Trailer
- ☐ Motorhome
- ☐ Tarps
- ☐ Tents

- ☐ Shelter-Making Skills and Knowledge
- ☐ _____
- ☐ _____
- ☐ _____
- ☐ _____
- ☐ _____

First Aid and Health

In survival situations, there are 5 things pertaining to first aid you'll want in place: first aid skills/knowledge, supplies and medications, the ability to replenish supplies and medications, and books or manuals to teach you what you don't already know. You should also list who in your area has the medical expertise you don't have, so you can go to them for help, if needed.

Also, how will you stay healthy long-term. Do you have exercise equipment, running shoes, sports equipment, or other items available that will allow you to build your endurance and keep your body strong and healthy during a long-term crisis?

Here are some ideas you can consider:

First-Aid and Health Ideas – Keep your health up, especially when you need it most.

☐ The Survival Medicine Handbook
☐ Home Remedies Medicine Book
☐ First-Aid or EMT Training
☐ CPR/AED Certification
☐ Connections to Doctors, Dentists, Etc.
☐ First-Aid Manuals
☐ Small, Portable First-Aid Kit
☐ Larger, More Complete First-Aid Kit
☐ Splints, Braces, and Crutches
☐ Alcohol, Hydrogen Peroxide, Ointments
☐ Super Glue to Suture Large Cuts
☐ Several Types of Bandages
☐ Tweezers, Scissors, and Other Tools
☐ Stethoscope
☐ Blood-Pressure Cuff
☐ Breathing Apparatuses (OPAs, BVMs, etc.)
☐ Mosquito/Bug Repellant
☐ Chewable Aspirin, Nitroglycerine
☐ Injectable Epinephrine
☐ Rehydration Salts/Electrolytes
☐ Extra Medications (Prescription, etc.)
☐ Israeli Bandages
☐ Tourniquets
☐ QuikClot
☐ _____
☐ _____

☐ Pull-up Bar
☐ Sports Equipment, Balls, Etc.
☐ Yoga Matt
☐ Weights or Weight-Lifting Equipment
☐ Exercise Bands
☐ Exercise Ball
☐ Foam Roller
☐ Mini-Trampoline
☐ Exercise Clothes and Shoes
☐ Treadmill, Bike, or Cardio Equipment
☐ Jump Rope
☐ _____
☐ _____
☐ _____
☐ _____
☐ _____
☐ _____
☐ _____
☐ _____
☐ _____
☐ _____
☐ _____
☐ _____
☐ _____
☐ _____

Communication

During worst-case or long-term emergencies, how will you keep in touch with others, listen to the news, or let others know you need help? Here are some ideas below:

Communication Ideas – Listen to the news and keep in contact with others.

☐ Ham Radios and Ham Radio Skills	☐ Signaling Mirror
☐ Portable AM/FM Radio	☐ Laser Pointer
☐ Two-Way Radios (Walkie Talkies)	☐ Flashlights
☐ Red (or Other) Paint and Poster Boards	☐ _____
☐ Whistle or Horn	☐ _____
☐ Flares or Flare Gun	☐ _____
☐ Emergency Signs (Including Bright Colors)	☐ _____

Sanitation, Hygiene, and Disposal

During a crisis, disease can spread quickly if you can't flush toilets, dispose of trash, disinfect surfaces, or bathe. Without a good plan for sanitation, hygiene, and disposal, things can go from ugly to much uglier, quickly. See below for some ideas and suggestions:

Sanitation & Hygiene Ideas – Germs can spread fast in crisis. Keep clean!

☐ Clean Water (Wash Hands & Clean Often)	☐ Cleaning Supplies/Chemicals
☐ Dental Hygiene (Toothpaste, Brushes, Etc.)	☐ Sponges, Scrubbing Pads, Dish Towels
☐ Lots of Soap (Kitchen Soap, Bar Soap, Etc.)	☐ Drying Rack
☐ Septic Tank and Supplies	☐ Buckets for Sewage Transport/Disposal
☐ Extra Supply of Trash Bags	☐ Two Bucket System (Urine vs Feces)
☐ Compost Pile/Bin	☐ Calcium Hypochlorite (for Sanitation)
☐ Surgical Gloves	☐ Tissues
☐ Portable Shower	☐ Hand Sanitizers
☐ Shampoos/Conditioners	☐ Cat Litter, Sawdust, Shredded Paper, etc.
☐ Toilet Paper, LOTS of Toilet Paper ☺	☐ Humanure Handbook
☐ Feminine Hygiene Needs	☐ _____
☐ Infant Hygiene Needs	☐ _____
☐ Manual Clothes Washer	☐ _____
☐ Laundry Detergent	☐ _____
☐ Clothes Lines (for Drying Clothes, Etc.)	☐ _____

Transportation

In a difficult crisis, fossil fuels might be hard to get, or your car might stop working. How will you and your family get from place to place or transport needed supplies from location to location? Here are a few ideas to consider:

Transportation Ideas – How would you get around if fuel was limited or non-existent?

- ☐ Bicycles (& Bicycle Trailers) & Extra Parts
- ☐ Moped, Scooter, Motorcycle
- ☐ ATV, Snowmobile, Off-Road Vehicles
- ☐ In-Line Skates or Skateboards
- ☐ Baby Strollers or Bicycle Baby Seats
- ☐ Baby Hiking Backpacks
- ☐ Powered Paraglider
- ☐ Wagon

- ☐ Kayak, Canoe, Boat, or Rowboat
- ☐ Horses, Donkeys, or Other Animals
- ☐ Snowshoes, Skis, Snowboard
- ☐ _____
- ☐ _____
- ☐ _____
- ☐ _____
- ☐ _____

Self-Defense and Safety

When people can't feed themselves or their children, they sometimes do desperate things. You're always 72 hours away from a riot. Get prepared with skills, weapons (which can double up for hunting), and tools to protect yourself and your loved ones from anything dangerous.

Self-Defense & Safety Ideas – Protect from other people, from animals, situations, etc.

- ☐ Guns and Ammunition
- ☐ Gun Cleaning Supplies
- ☐ Gun Vault or Safe
- ☐ Gun Scopes or Suppressors
- ☐ Mace or Pepper Spray
- ☐ Mace or Pepper Spray
- ☐ Hunting Knives
- ☐ Stun Gun or Taser
- ☐ Bow and Arrows
- ☐ Martial Arts Skills
- ☐ Wrestling Skills
- ☐ Bullet-proof Vest
- ☐ Brass Knuckles
- ☐ Sling Shots
- ☐ Dust or Surgical Masks

- ☐ Gas Masks
- ☐ Large Zip Ties (Good for Handcuffs Also)
- ☐ Goggles
- ☐ Ear Plugs
- ☐ Steel-Toed Boots
- ☐ Work Gloves
- ☐ Hard Hat
- ☐ Bright Clothes or Reflective Wear
- ☐ Camouflage Clothing
- ☐ _____
- ☐ _____
- ☐ _____
- ☐ _____
- ☐ _____
- ☐ _____

Entertainment and Education

During emotionally draining emergencies, how will you keep your minds engaged, your emotions positive, and stay socially connected? Here are some ideas to consider:

Entertainment & Education Ideas – Keep your mind engaged and socially connect.

- ☐ Books to Read and Learn From
- ☐ Journals and Pens
- ☐ Scriptures and Scripture Markers
- ☐ Board Games
- ☐ Card Games
- ☐ Dice
- ☐ Lawn Games and Frisbees
- ☐ Sports Equipment
- ☐ Storytelling Skills
- ☐ Crafts
- ☐ Musical Instruments and Sheet Music
- ☐ Portable Music (Harmonicas, iPod, Etc.)
- ☐ Songbooks for Singing
- ☐ Puppets
- ☐ Coloring and Painting Materials
- ☐ Puzzles and Puzzle Books
- ☐ Photo Albums
- ☐ Put on Your Own Plays
- ☐ _____
- ☐ _____

Practical Tools and Supplies

In worst case scenarios, how will repair your house or appliances? How will you build solutions to meet your life-saving needs? Crisis situations have the tendency to bring out the creative side in us. What tools and supplies will you need?

Extra Tools/Supplies Ideas – Extra tools or supplies that might save your life.

- ☐ Ax/Hatchet
- ☐ Hammers (regular, sledge, etc.)
- ☐ Pliers and Wrenches
- ☐ Saws (Chain, Circular, Hand, etc.)
- ☐ Nails and Screws
- ☐ Staple Guns and Staples
- ☐ Drills
- ☐ Picks
- ☐ Shovels
- ☐ Rakes
- ☐ Screwdrivers
- ☐ Wood and Wood Pieces
- ☐ Ropes, Cord, and Twine
- ☐ Duct and Other Tapes
- ☐ Glues
- ☐ Extra Wire and Electronics
- ☐ Electrical Repair Tools
- ☐ Extension Cords
- ☐ Gardening Tools and Supplies
- ☐ Work Gloves
- ☐ Wheel Barrel/Wagon
- ☐ Tarps/Coverings/Visqueen
- ☐ WD-40 and other lubricants
- ☐ Tools Chests or Tool Bags
- ☐ _____
- ☐ _____
- ☐ _____
- ☐ _____

Other Skills or Ideas

If there are other skills, items, or ideas you're interested in, but they weren't covered in the sections above, feel free to write them in the spaces below.

Extra Skills or Other Ideas

☐ _____   ☐ _____

☐ _____   ☐ _____

☐ _____   ☐ _____

☐ _____   ☐ _____

☐ _____   ☐ _____

☐ _____   ☐ _____

☐ _____   ☐ _____

☐ _____   ☐ _____

☐ _____   ☐ _____

☐ _____   ☐ _____

☐ _____   ☐ _____

☐ _____   ☐ _____

☐ _____   ☐ _____

☐ _____   ☐ _____

PrepStep #6
MAINTAIN STANDARDS OF LIVING

"Life should not be estimated exclusively by the standard of dollars and cents."
- *Charles Goodyear*

MAINTAIN STANDARDS OF LIVING

The ultimate goal of emergency preparedness is to be so prepared that when a crisis hits it doesn't seem like a crisis to you or your family.

To do this, there is another level of preparedness that few ever consider. It's the preparation you need to maintain your standards of living throughout the crisis.

For example, in extreme events such as hyperinflation or a large economic breakdown, how would you comfortably pass through the chaos?

To maintain your current standard of living, you'll need to ask yourself, "How can I preserve my savings if my country's currency lost its complete value?" and also ask, "If I couldn't go shopping for a year or more, would I have everything I need to live comfortably at home during that time?"

Part of *real* preparation is knowing that you're completely self-sufficient (at least for a short while) and ready for all types of emergencies that may come your way.

SET YOUR "STANDARD-OF-LIVING" PREPAREDNESS GOAL DATES:

✓ Create a Rainy-Day Fund. (Goal Date: _____)

✓ Create A Hedge Against Inflation. (Goal Date: _____)

✓ Gather and Store Up Extra Supplies. (Goal Date: _____)

Goal 1: Create a Rainy-Day Fund

During a crisis, banks may close or go offline, or you may find yourself not able to use credit cards like you normally do. For those occasions, keep some extra cash on hand, just in case.

Everyone has different needs, so obviously how much money to store is up to you. I recommend at least 30 days' worth set aside as your "rainy-day" fund to pay your bills. Hopefully even more. You'll be glad you did.

This is a fund you can use and borrow from anytime you find yourself in a pinch, but it should be replenished immediately, since it's primarily for emergency situations.

Make sure your fund is made up of smaller bills and even coins. Here in the United States, I especially like to have mostly $1 bills and also some $5 and $10 ones, but not many $20+ notes. The smaller the note, the easier it is to trade for what you might need, without giving away too much of your rainy-day fund unnecessarily. Not everyone will have (or offer) change back.

Your rainy-day fund should be stored nearby you (and not in the bank). You want it easily accessible and in actual cash (not stock, etc.). It should be very "liquid."

You can get really creative when it comes to deciding where you hide your rainy-day fund. Remember that under your bed, in drawers, and in the closet are "obvious" places. Think of places most people wouldn't consider or places that are difficult to get to. Here are a couple of suggestions:

- In an envelope taped to the bottom of a kitchen or bathroom cabinet, a dresser drawer, toy box, a bookshelf, a potted plant, or even your kitty's litter box.
- In an envelope taped to the back of a painting or other wall decoration.
- In a watertight plastic bottle or jar inside the tank of your toilet.
- In a plastic bag inside your refrigerator/freezer.
- Inside a container of beans or quick oats.
- Inside a sock in your sock drawer
- Inside a hollowed-out book on your shelves.
- In an empty aspirin or other bottle in your medicine cabinet.
- In the pocket of a particular pair of pants or shirt you don't use very often.
- In a utility closet (away from the furnace, of course, haha).
- In the rafters
- Under a removable floorboard.

Like I mentioned, it's always good to have at least a month's worth of extra cash on hand at all times, yet there's one more thing to consider. If things get really tough, people will turn to a barter system (you know, like in the old days). "I'll give you some batteries for a pound of butter," right!?

So, as part of my rainy-day fund, I like to keep a few non-perishable "tradable" items stored away as well. I suggest you do the same.

Goal 2: Create a Hedge Against Inflation

BRAZIL 1989-1990 I lived in Brazil back in 1989 and 1990 during some of the worst inflation in Brazil's history. In 1989 the inflation rate was about 1400% and in 1990 it jumped up to over 30,000%.

What that means, in simple terms, is that if you had $30,000 at the beginning of 1990, it would be worth $1 by the end of the year.

To keep up with the devaluation, the currency in Brazil needed to be modified and reprinted several times.

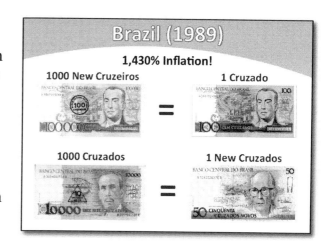

Over that 2-year period, the Brazil currency went from Cruzeiros to Cruzados, and then from Cruzados to New Cruzados, and then eventually went back to Cruzeiros for the 3rd time in Brazil's history.

Living through that type of inflation was an educational experience for me, to say the least. Yet, my experience was different from every Brazilian around me, because I had dollars to trade and they didn't.

At the time, the American dollar was probably the most secure and stable currency in the world. If a Brazilian could get a hold of dollars, he would use those as his "hedge" against inflation. So, it was pretty easy to exchange dollars any time I wanted to! ☺

What that means is that 10 Cruzeiros at the beginning of the month might be worth 1 Cruzeiro at the end of the month, but 1 Dollar at the beginning of the month was still worth the same 1 Dollar by the end. That 1 dollar could then be traded in for 100 Cruzeiros instead. No value lost. Make sense?

In other words, the Brazilian who traded his paycheck for dollars would still have the same buying power (maybe more) by the end of the month, while others around him were forced to spend all their Cruzeiros in a hurry or their money would soon be worthless.

In 1990, buying dollars was a great way to preserve wealth and ride out inflation in Brazil, but what do we do if what happened in Brazil happens in the United States?

In the first 2 decades of the 21st century, the United States more than quadrupled its national debt to well over 23 trillion dollars. Then, the 2020 COVID-19 pandemic hit, and our nation's debt grew more in one year than any time in U.S. history. Coupling that with all the nation's unfunded liabilities (like Social Security), an out-of-control derivative market, an unstable world economy, and job insecurities, things have gone from bad to worse.

National economies can be fragile and sometimes it doesn't take much for them to fall apart, even the United States.

Venezuela, for example, had some of biggest oil reserves and was filled with valuable natural resources. Just a handful of decades ago, Venezuela was the 4th wealthiest country worldwide. Yet, in 2015, Venezuela spiraled out of control with less than 200 billion in national debt, experiencing over 50,000,000% inflation in a few short years. That pales my 30,000% Brazil inflation experience. ☺

This all happened while Venezuela had a population about 1/10th that of the United States. If you were to ten times what Venezuela owed in debt to equal the population of the United States, you'd see that Venezuela folded financially under the U.S. equivalent of nearly 2 trillion in debt (nothing compared to the size of the U.S. deficit).

144

Along with our country's astronomical debt, we also have a fragile credit system. More people live off credit today than any time in our history. All it would take is a sudden rise in interest rates or a large restriction in credit for our economy (and maybe our currency) to spiral uncontrollably downward.

In a way, the U.S. economy is following some of the same pathways that Brazil and Venezuela followed before inflation hit them hard. Yet, the United States has found "security" in being the world's reserve currency and the petrol dollar. Since we've been in a position to gain more than any other country, we also have just as much to lose.

In Brazil, the dollar was probably the most popular hedge against inflation in 1990. But how do you hedge against inflation when your currency *is* the dollar, and the dollar falls apart?

CREATING YOUR HEDGE

In 1965, minimum wage was $1.25 an hour (or 5 silver quarters). At today's standards, $1.25 doesn't go far. If I were your employer and only paid you $1.25 an hour, you'd feel cheated, and I'd soon face a judge in court, I'm sure.

But what if I paid you 5 silver quarters instead? Would you be happy? You should be! You'd be making much more than minimum wage. Isn't that funny? It's still 5 quarters. The difference is that silver retains its value over time and makes up for inflation. It's similar to how the dollar remained stable while the Brazilian currency lost its value quickly.

There are several ways to hedge (or protect) the value of your money. Some people prefer land, some copper, some gold, but I prefer silver.

I'm not a financial consultant (that was my disclaimer!), but in my opinion, though a little volatile, silver is one of the best hedges against inflation that I know.

Silver is an industrial metal so it will always be needed for production. But it's also considered poor man's gold since it's much cheaper to buy an ounce of silver than it is to buy an ounce of gold. In a crisis, that means it's easier to buy, sell, or trade smaller-value currencies like silver, than more expensive ones, like gold.

Also, historically silver has better growth margins than gold. If gold spikes up quickly, silver spikes up even quicker. That means that investment ratios tend to favor silver during economically challenged times.

However, you'll want to make sure you have physical silver (not paper or investment silver) on hand. And, just like your rainy-day fund, you'll want your silver easily accessible and well hidden in your possession, not in a 3rd-party vault. If things got bad enough, you might never see your silver again if it's housed outside your immediate control.

But how do you get silver? Silver can be bought and sold at coin or precious-metal dealers in most any city, or you can buy it online and have it shipped to you. Be careful with some pawnshops or with private purchases. Make sure you're getting a fair price and you're actually getting real silver, inside and out.

When you purchase silver, you want to make sure it was either minted by the United States itself (or other well-known country) or by a well-known and respected mine or dealer. If it's minted by a well-respected mine, then make sure all your silver coins or bars have "999" or "9999" fine silver on them. Some coin dealers will refuse to buy them from you, unless it specifically states its purity.

There are 3 types of silver that I prefer to buy. I'll list them here in priority, from my personal favorite to my least favorite:

1. **Silver Eagles**. 1 troy ounce Silver American Eagles are as pure as silver gets and are easily recognizable. Dealers have no problem recognizing their value or buying them back. Also, the general public doesn't have to question whether or not this U.S. coin is actually silver or not, because it says "fine silver" very clearly on the back.

   Silver Eagles usually come at a premium price, so don't expect to pay "spot" (or market) price for them. These are my favorite because they are always in demand by coin dealers when other forms of silver may not be, especially in a crisis.

2. **Junk Silver.** These are typically U.S. minted coins before 1965 and typically contain 90% silver in them, rather than pure silver. The most popular are the half-dollars and the quarters, but some people also get a mixture of dimes in their collection as well.

It's called "junk" silver, not because it's old and looks like junk, but because it doesn't have any "collectable" value above the actual silver the coin contains. In other words, rare coin collectors aren't that interested in these coins.

It's good to have a fair supply of these on hand as well as American Eagles. It creates variety.

The price of these coins is determined by what is called the "melt value" of the silver. The melt value is how much people would pay for that silver if the coin was melted down and only the silver remained.

Junk silver is a good investment because it usually costs less than silver American Eagles, yet people still recognize the coin easily as a U.S. minted coin.

The problem is that most people (except for dealers, of course) don't know or remember that coins minted prior to 1965 were mostly silver. You may have to do some educating or convincing on the spot in an emergency. Junk silver coins don't contain the words "silver" on them like American Eagles or other silver coins and bars do.

3. **Silver Bars.** My 3rd favorite way of buying silver is in bars, again for variety sake.

   Silver bars are typically minted by mines and for some reason people tend to believe bars are actually made of silver more than they believe generic silver coins (called "silver rounds") are.

   My recommendation is that if you do buy silver bars, don't get anything heavier than 10 ounces per bar. Even though 100 or 1000-ounce bars are still easy to trade with a dealer, during a crisis, if you can't get to a dealer, you may find it difficult to sell a silver bar worth over $1000 to the general public.

When it comes to figuring out how much silver to buy, you'll have to decide what works best for you. I recommend, if it's in your budget, that you store at least a year's worth of mortgage (or rent), utilities, and expenses on hand in silver.

If putting away that much silver seems impossible to you right now, at least get what you can afford. Something is better than nothing, right?!

Storing away plenty of silver will help you feel peace and security now and in the future. If hyperinflation did someday hit you, or you lost your job, or food and gas prices suddenly rose, you would have enough of a hedge against inflation (and a good savings plan) in place to protect yourself and your family for a while. You could get through the tough times without losing your shirt (literally).

Since your silver is for long-term storage and future protection (rather than a shorter-term investment), don't worry if the price of silver fluctuates up or down a little here and there, month after month or year after year. Buy it, put it away, and forget about it, until you really need it.

One more piece of advice: if you're concerned about anonymity, make sure you buy your silver from a dealer in person. Don't pay more than $9,999.99 in cash for your silver at a time. When you purchase $10,000 in silver or more, even with cash, dealers may be required to keep and submit a record of your purchase.

Goal 3: Gather and Store Up Extra Supplies

Typically, in the preparedness industry, maintaining your standard of living isn't addressed, but for your emotional welfare (your sanity) during a long-term crisis, it's a great practice to implement. Why not thrive, not just survive, through an emergency?

After experiencing 30,000% inflation in Brazil in 1990, I learned a big lesson. I would rather buy extra supplies from the store today while they're available, inexpensive, and I have the money to do so, rather than wait until shelves are emptied or prices too high to afford.

But, what should you buy then? Here's a little exercise to find out...

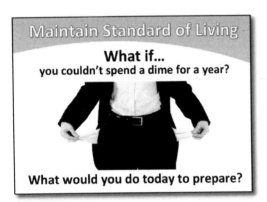

Imagine that somehow your food, your mortgage/rent, and your utilities were paid off for a year ahead of time. And, now imagine that you didn't even have a dime to spend on anything else for that whole year.

What would you have bought *ahead of time* (and stored away) in order to make that year more comfortable for you and your family? How would you make sure you could maintain your standards of living during those 12 months as much as possible?

When my wife and I first did this, we began by making a list of everything we spend money on in a typical year. Ideas would pop into our minds in the middle of the day and the night, and we would write them down. It took us weeks to create that list, but it was well worth it.

We walked around stores (like supermarkets, Costco, and hardware stores), and jotted down our thoughts. It was a great exercise! (I recommend you do that as well.)

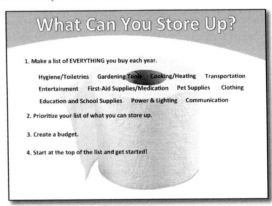

We then ended up buying extra clothes (even shoelaces) and storing them away. The same with toilet paper, soap, shampoo, lotion, feminine items, razors, cotton swabs, gardening supplies, paper products, pens, and more.

It's comforting to know, after all that work, that if a major crisis did hit, we'd be comfortable for a long time. (To help you save time, I've included much of our list on the following page.)

MAKING YOUR LIST AND PRIORITIZING IT

To help maintain your standard of living during a long-term crisis, create a list of everything you'd normally spend money on within a typical year, just like we did. Then, as your budget allows, purchase a little extra each time you shop. On the following page are some suggestions to begin with, but feel free to add to the list.

Gather and Store Extra Supplies

- ☐ Combs, Hairbrush, Curlers, Bobby Pins
- ☐ Hairspray, Gel, or Paste
- ☐ Shampoo and Conditioner
- ☐ Haircutting Kit
- ☐ Hair Colors/Dyes/Highlights
- ☐ Toothpaste
- ☐ Toothbrushes
- ☐ Tongue Scrapers
- ☐ Mouthwash
- ☐ Dental Floss or Picks
- ☐ Razor Blades
- ☐ Shaving Cream
- ☐ Wash Towels or Rags
- ☐ Facial Tissues
- ☐ Makeup, Tweezers, etc.
- ☐ Extra Glasses, Contacts, Saline Solution
- ☐ Contraceptives
- ☐ Feminine Hygiene
- ☐ Toilet Paper
- ☐ Bar Soap and Hand Sanitizers
- ☐ Lotion
- ☐ Deodorant
- ☐ Diapers
- ☐ Infant Hygiene
- ☐ Paper Plates, Cups
- ☐ Plastic Utensils
- ☐ Dish Soap
- ☐ Ziploc Baggies and Food Containers
- ☐ Trash Bags
- ☐ Aluminum Foil
- ☐ Saran Wrap
- ☐ Paper Towels
- ☐ Water Softener Salts/Filters
- ☐ Spices
- ☐ Sponges and Scrubbing Pads
- ☐ Detergents and Cleaning Supplies
- ☐ Pet Food
- ☐ Pet Toys
- ☐ Pet Grooming Kits & Shampoo

- ☐ Laundry Detergent and Softeners
- ☐ Spray and Wash
- ☐ Dryer Sheets
- ☐ Pants or Shorts
- ☐ Shirts
- ☐ Winter Clothes
- ☐ Summer Clothes
- ☐ Business Clothes
- ☐ Church Clothes
- ☐ Exercise or Sports Clothes
- ☐ Underwear (Including Bras)
- ☐ Shoes/Footwear (Including Shoelaces)
- ☐ Socks and Nylons
- ☐ Shoeshine Kit
- ☐ Hats, Beanies, Earmuffs, Headwear
- ☐ Bicycle Spare Parts & Repair Kits
- ☐ Bike Tires, Inner Tubes, Pump
- ☐ Car or Motorcycle Supplies
- ☐ Seeds
- ☐ Garden Supplies
- ☐ Extra Fuel (Wood, Propane, Charcoal, ...)
- ☐ Batteries
- ☐ Candles
- ☐ Medications/First Aid
- ☐ Alcohol, Cotton Swabs, Q-tips
- ☐ Hydrogen Peroxide
- ☐ Band-Aids and Bandages
- ☐ Allergy Medications
- ☐ Chapstick or Lip Balm
- ☐ Sun Block or Tanning Lotion
- ☐ Work Tools/Supplies (Nails, Screws, ...)
- ☐ Pens, Pencils, Rubber Bands, Paper Clips
- ☐ Paper and Folders
- ☐ Backpacks
- ☐ Ink Cartridges
- ☐ Holiday Supplies
- ☐ House Plant Supplies
- ☐ Light Bulbs
- ☐ Guitar Strings

PrepStep #7
HELP OTHERS GET PREPARED

"Your own safety is at stake when your neighbor's wall is ablaze."
-- *Horace*

HELP OTHERS GET PREPARED

Brains!! BRAAAAIINNNS!!!! Have you ever noticed how in zombie movies, the zombies' meal of choice is other people? Zombies live off of others! Hmmm, maybe it can become truer than we think.

As the final step of The 7 Prep Steps, you need to understand that what others around you do (or don't do) to prepare for emergencies, affects you. If you're the only one prepared in a neighborhood, who do you think desperate people will come to in order to survive, if things get really out of control?

Since unprepared people, in a way, can become zombies and eat off of YOU, you should create a "No Zombies" rule by helping others get prepared around you.

I'm not saying unprepared people will eat your brains (well, maybe they will), but it's really difficult to say "no!" to someone you care about when you have food and supplies, and they don't.

I'm a bit of a softie myself, and I tend to store more than I need to because I know not all my neighbors *will* get prepared. As one food storage expert says, "I've got 2 years supply, one for my family, and one for all the people who will be knocking on my door for help."

The sad truth is few people will ever get prepared without a little nudging from friends or family first. To conclude this workbook, I leave you with your final 2 goals:

SET YOUR "HELP OTHERS GET PREPARED" GOAL DATES:

- ✓ Create a List of Family, Friends, and Neighbors to Help. (Goal Date: _____)

- ✓ Reach Out to the People on Your List and Help Them. (Goal Date: _____)

Goal 1: Create a List of Family, Friends, and Neighbors

Make a list of family, friends, and neighbors around you (at church, at school, at work, etc.), and also make a list of family members and close friends that may not be living nearby. For your emotional welfare, it feels good to know people you care about, even far away, are safe during a crisis.

After you make your list, prioritize it. As you do so, you may want to give extra consideration to the people who are least prepared or who you care about the most. You can also prioritize your list by picking out leaders who have the gift or ability to motivate others easily. Get them on board and your job gets a lot easier.

Family and Relatives:

☐ _____   ☐ _____

☐ _____   ☐ _____

☐ _____   ☐ _____

☐ _____   ☐ _____

☐ _____   ☐ _____

☐ _____   ☐ _____

☐ _____   ☐ _____

☐ _____   ☐ _____

Friends, Neighbors, and Coworkers:

☐ _____   ☐ _____

☐ _____   ☐ _____

☐ _____   ☐ _____

☐ _____   ☐ _____

☐ _____   ☐ _____

☐ _____   ☐ _____

☐ _____   ☐ _____

☐ _____   ☐ _____

Leaders and Influencers

☐ _____   ☐ _____

☐ _____   ☐ _____

☐ _____   ☐ _____

☐ _____   ☐ _____

Goal 2: Reach Out and Help Others Get Prepared

Now that you've prioritized your list, it's time to make a difference and reach out. Start at the top and begin sharing the principles you learned in this book with those you care about.

Remember to not pressure or "sell" people on preparedness. If you pressure someone, they'll probably close off to any future help. My advice is to find something in preparedness they're interested in and share it with them to see if they're ready to learn more.

My neighbors know that I do emergency preparedness, and I've noticed that they approach me when they're ready. They don't feel pressured by me. Because of that, I've been able to help so many more people.

If it helps make your job easier, give them a copy of the 7PrepSteps workbook or have them access the 7PrepSteps online course. They'll be able to learn the right information at their own pace.

Also, remember the power of leveraging influencers or leaders in your neighborhood, community, church, or at work. Since they have positions of authority, they can help you motivate several people at one time.

In any case, do yourself a favor and help others get prepared. You'll gain not only peace of mind but also the gratitude of your neighbors and loved ones.

CONGRATULATIONS! You Completed The 7 Prep Steps!!